S0-BZZ-757

Are You Sure You're the PRINCIPAL?

For Evan, my son, and Adria, my daughter:
I love you *this much*, "just because."

Are You Sure You're the PRINCIPAL?

On Being an Authentic Leader

Susan Villani

Foreword by Roland S. Barth

CORWIN PRESS, INC.
A Sage Publications Company
Thousand Oaks, California

For information address:

Corwin Press, Inc.
A Sage Publications Company
2455 Teller Road
Thousand Oaks, California 91320
E-mail: order@corwinpress.com

SAGE Publications Ltd.
6 Bonhill Street
London EC2A 4PU
United Kingdom

SAGE Publications India Pvt. Ltd.
M-32 Market
Greater Kailash I
New Delhi 110 048 India

Printed in the United States of America

Library of Congress Cataloging-in-Publication Data

Villani, Susan.
    Are you sure you're the principal? : On being an authentic leader /
Susan Villani.
        p. cm.

    ISBN 0-8039-6804-3 (cloth: acid-free paper)
    ISBN 0-8039-6805-1 (pbk.: acid-free paper)
    1. School principals—United States. 2. Women school principals—United States.
3. Educational leadership—United States. I. Title.
    LB2831.92 .V55 1999
    371.2'012—dc21
                                                99-6253

99 00 01 02 03 04 05 10 9 8 7 6 5 4 3 2 1

Production Editor: S. Marlene Head
Typesetter: Technical Typesetting, Inc.
Cover Designer: Ravi Balasuriya

Contents

Foreword

The knowledge base for improving schools is thought to reside in large-scale social science research. When policymakers in Sacramento, Tallahassee, or Washington want to know what is right or wrong with public schools, what should be changed, and how school leaders should accomplish this, they turn to the work of a Ron Edmonds or a John Goodlad.

There is another knowledge base of inestimable value to the improvement of public schools. This "literature" is much less evident than formal research in discussions about school reform. Craft knowledge is the massive collection of experiences and learnings that those who live and work under the roof of the schoolhouse inevitably amass during their careers. These are the insights garnered by teachers, principals, guidance counselors, librarians, school secretaries, and parents about important matters such as parent involvement, staff development, curriculum development, discipline, teaching, leadership, and school improvement.

Tragically, the wisdom from the craft rarely is viewed—by outsiders or by school people themselves—as legitimate or rigorous, let alone useful, to the important work of school improvement. I believe there are three reasons why this happens: First, when a fourth-grade teacher or a principal speaks, it is believed that out will come, not craft knowledge, but a war story. "Let me tell you about the time I tried to fire a teacher . . ." Eyes glaze over.

War stories are descriptions of practice, verbal portraits of the events of the schoolhouse. Craft knowledge is description of practice accompanied by analysis of practice. "Let me tell you about the time I tried to fire a teacher—and here's what I learned from it. If I were to do it again, here's how I would do it differently." These hardwon learnings from practice are the gold of the realm.

Second, in the cruel world of schools, which places practitioners in the position of competitor with others for scarce recognition and resources, few are willing to share their gold, panned from years of experience, lest their fellows come to occupy a position of greater respect and admiration.

Finally, even if a teacher or principal chooses to, it is often not safe for a practitioner to disclose his or her craft knowledge to fellow educators. This is likely to be greeted in a faculty room with put-downs: "Big deal. I've been doing that for years."

Thus, our profession seems to neither welcome nor value either the giving or the receiving of craft knowledge. What a tragic loss to the profession, to the professionals, and to the cause of school reform.

I recently completed and published a collection of stories about my many years sailing the coast of Maine. In the course of writing this book, I have come to learn something of the extraordinary power of storytelling and the gifts that it can bring to the teller and the audience alike.

Additionally, I am discovering that storytelling may provide an important key, capable of unlocking the wisdom of the educational, as well as the nautical, craft.

Susan Villani has discovered this key as well. She tells us that "we need to hear more stories about leadership." The book you are about to read is replete with stories and vignettes from her 20-year career as a public school principal. Embedded in them is a treasure trove of craft knowledge. Her learnings on the job, courageously disclosed, become strikingly accessible, useful, and even healing for aspiring and practicing principals alike.

I think you will find this collection of stories, and the analysis that accompanies each, deeply personal, engaging, and introspective. Above all, you will find that through storytelling, Susan Villani brings an abundance of "authenticity."

Enjoy, and make wise use of the gift of the hardwon wisdom offered by this accomplished and reflective practitioner.

ROLAND S. BARTH
Founding Director,
Harvard Principals' Center

Preface

The Leadership Dilemma

Our schools need leaders who have vision and are prepared to act on it—leaders who continually promote growth and explore alternative approaches to learning, community building, problem solving, and teacher empowerment. When we find creative, talented, and visionary leaders, we want them to be everything they are and use everything they know to do their work.

Sometimes, when leaders share more of themselves, people may feel confused and even threatened. Although leaders often are chosen because of their personal traits, when they act authentically (genuinely sharing themselves), the school community may critique and try to modify the very attributes that distinguished them.

This book serves to encourage and support leaders in being authentic and to educate school communities about effective leadership. It is important for staff, teachers, administrators, families, and the larger community to understand that to be effective, leaders must lead in their own ways—and that the resulting changes in the schools are in the service of promoting an even better education for all students. When people understand this, they will be even more inclined to work through their differences, pooling talents and resources in the spirit of working together.

Mentoring Through Stories

I wish there had been a book like this when I first became a principal—a book in which an experienced leader shared her or his craft wisdom in a personal way, through stories. My book is unique because it is one principal's stories and reflections over the course of a 20-year career. It chronicles my path in leadership, from the excruciating challenges of my first year as a principal, to becoming an effective and respected leader, a trainer of leaders, and a leader of a leadership organization.

Reading my book is like sitting with an experienced colleague and hearing some ways that she makes sense of her practice. One contribution to educational administration is that this book illustrates leadership that is authentic. By telling stories, I reveal who I am, what I believe, and what I've hoped for, struggled with, and achieved. Through stories, ideas about leadership are more accessible to readers interested in the practical as well as the theoretical.

The ways we have experienced direction, guidance, and authority are connected to the leaders we become. My stories illustrate the kind of self-reflection that may inspire readers to explore past and present influences on their own thinking. Understanding the links between influences on our leadership and our current practice may lead to an exploration of the nuances and variations of our craft—thereby elevating it to the art of leadership—and that's where more growth is always possible.

Organization

Two organizing principles structure this book. The core issues of leadership are illustrated and discussed through stories, while the evolution of a leader, over time, also is portrayed. To punctuate the stories and commentary, artwork, dialogue, correspondence, and other writings are included.

Who's Who in Readership

Practicing administrators and school leaders will readily identify with the issues presented in this book, and may also resonate with the feelings that accompany them. Parents are often curious about the schools their children attend and welcome more insight into school management and leadership. Aspiring administrators need to be exposed to a variety of ways of leading in order to discover what is congruent with their values and educational philosophy. They are concerned most with the challenges facing principals and will value the candid discussion of real-life situations. Anyone interested in women's experiences or a relational approach to leadership will find these stories engaging, whether the reflections affirm or inform the reader's own thinking. Leaders in other fields, such as business, will benefit from this book; seeing leadership in another context provides a way to clarify and expand their concept of leadership. In addition, whereas everyone has strong opinions about schools, these stories offer a powerful invitation for all readers to rethink education.

Chapter 1: A New Person in an Old Role: Multiple Images of a Principal

I have never believed in stereotypes. I have fought against them my whole life. However, if you had asked me when I first became a principal to describe a leader, a stereotypical character would have emerged. It would have been someone who acted and influenced, someone who commanded respect. It would have been a prominent presence whose opinions were known, a person who could handle any situation.

This first chapter is about coming to terms with stereotypes and distortions, beginning with my own. These stories are about learning that regardless of what I presented, people's expectations of me have altered their perceptions. My early experiences as a principal confirmed that becoming the educational leader of a school involves a lot more than simply being appointed to the position.

Chapter 2: Working Through Conflict: Power and Communication

The stories in this chapter are about conflict, communication, and the effect of power on both. Even though I could teach students ways to resolve conflicts with their peers, it was much more difficult to identify, understand, and work through the conflicts I was having with staff members. Some of our interactions were excruciating.

Authentic ways to lead are not always welcomed or understood. Conflict, isolation, and group dynamics have, at times, undermined, but also strengthened, my resolve to become a respected presence in the school community. There is also the possibility for us to model, for children and adults, what we value.

Chapter 3: Being a Leader and Being Myself: Feelings, Attitudes, and Roles

In 20 years as a principal, I have found myself in many roles within the school system. Because I intuitively knew the importance of authenticity in leadership, I made a commitment to genuinely share my own feelings and thought processes. I moved from trying to fix things alone to helping groups of people find their own solutions, trusting in the importance of process. I learned to facilitate interactions and empowered school members to be involved in problem solving and decision making. This focus on empowerment and innovation is what moves us beyond management, to leadership that inspires.

Chapter 4: What We Have to Offer: Fitting a School Together

The stories in this chapter are about the people in our school community and how my leadership affected the ways we formed trusting and respectful relationships with each other. In so doing, we felt safe to take risks, explore individuals' interests, and experiment with innovative approaches to solving problems. I focused on bringing our community and diverse staff together to articulate and work toward an evolving vision for our school. Then my growth as a leader who was more comfortable expressing herself authentically and the school community's growth in collaboration created a synergy.

Chapter 5: Promoting Acceptance in the School Community: Each Person's Right to Belong

We all need recognition and acceptance. Even as a young student, I confused achievement with acceptance. I drove myself to accomplish more and more in an effort to ensure that I would belong, believing that I would be accepted for what I did, not for the person I was. The stories in this chapter reflect what I have done as a leader to help others learn about self-acceptance and acceptance of others. I believe we can only feel secure about our sense of belonging and acceptance if we know that we and others have shown ourselves authentically. When that happens, we can trust our community and feel free to pursue learning and achievement for our own growth.

Chapter 6: Mentors, Allies, and Friends: Support for Authentic Leadership and Vision

The stories in this chapter are about guidance, support, and affirmation. Being reminded of our traits and abilities can keep us from getting bogged down by confusion and self-doubt in challenging times. For beginners, mentors are invaluable teachers and supporters. However, even experienced leaders need to be validated, to seek support, and to recognize and accept it when it is offered. The fulfillment that comes to those who mentor is often one of the most rewarding aspects of their careers. Taking the next steps in our evolution as leaders and encouraging others to do the same is how we pass the torch to sustain leadership that is authentic.

Acknowledgments

It is with great affection that I acknowledge my father, Jerry Villani, and the memory of my grandmother, Catherine Villani, for their ongoing love, support, and belief in me. I thank Greta Morrine, my teacher at age 10, who made us write a story every day. At the time,

I panicked and cried each night, certain that I couldn't do it, but my mother sat with me and advised me to "write it just as you would say it." For such good advice, which still serves me well, and for countless hours at the kitchen table, I fondly remember my mother, Helen Hartzman Villani. Additionally, I thank Mr. Burns, who signaled to me that my writing was worth sharing with more people when he chose my essay for the high school yearbook.

When I accepted an invitation from Lesley College to be in a writing group for principals who had taken administrative interns, it was with Sharon Lowenstein, our group leader, that I first began to work on this book. I benefited tremendously from Sharon's undivided attention and guidance.

Laura Kranis was my writing coach as I wrote more stories, made a proposal to book publishers, and then created this book. Laura's thought-provoking questions led me to deeper understandings about my experiences and myself, and through her coaching I was able to improve my writing. For skills, for affirmation, and even for marathon coaching sessions, I am appreciative.

There were six people who read and reread my manuscript and gave me invaluable feedback and suggestions. Their insights strongly contributed to the quality of my work. My deeply felt gratitude goes to Nancy Bronson, Marlyn Miller, Susan Zellman-Rohrer, Mary Sterling, G. Huntington Damon, my father-in-law, and Henry Damon, my husband. Henry also showed his support in many other ways, including running 100 feet of electrical cord down to the dock at Squam Lake so I could write outdoors, making more than his share of suppers, and helping me to clarify my thinking about authenticity.

Receiving a phone call from Gracia Alkema, the president of Corwin Press, two weeks after I sent her a book proposal, was a respectful and warm welcome to publishing. Robb Clouse, the acquisitions editor who led me through the process of publishing this book, has been thoughtful about my work and most kind. I am thankful for their nurturing and encouragement.

The physical process of writing includes sitting for long periods of time. This can be a strain on one's body. I am thankful for the work Dr. Mary Benkert did to help keep my spine aligned as I worked long hours writing at the computer. As I prepared my manuscript, I appreciated technical assistance from Sue Howard, Maria Schofield, and Genoveva Matheus.

I've acknowledged some of the people who influenced me and supported my writing, and the people who directly helped me make this book be my very best. How do I express my appreciation for the impact of so many others throughout my life? To my family, friends, colleagues, instructors, students, and their families, who have taught, guided, challenged, mentored, taken a chance on, helped, accepted, valued, and encouraged me—to all of them, my heartfelt appreciation.

SUSAN VILLANI

About the Author

Susan Villani knows about being a principal because she has been one for 21 years. She has been the principal of schools with K–5, K–6, and 5–6 grade-level configurations, in three school districts, in two states. In her first year as a principal, she was named Young Career Woman of the Year by the Business and Professional Women's Association.

Not long after, Villani was elected president of the NorthEast Coalition of Educational Leaders (NECEL) and served on the board of directors for 6 years. She has taught graduate classes, spoken at conferences and meetings throughout the Northeast on leadership issues, coached aspiring administrators, and directed a résumé assessment service. Her doctoral dissertation was on mentoring, and she has consulted with school systems to establish mentoring programs for new teachers.

Villani was commissioned by the Rhode Island Department of Education to write about programs on cultural awareness and career exploration that she codeveloped. Her articles on mentoring have appeared in publications by the Principals' Center at Harvard and the University of Massachusetts. Villani wrote "A Principal Defined" in *Out of Women's Experience*, by Helen Regan and Gwen Brooks

(1995, Corwin Press), and she chaired the writing of the position paper of the Massachusetts Elementary School Principals' Association on prejudice and stereotyping.

Villani takes inspiration from the turtle: You have to stick your neck out to move forward.

Introduction

This book chronicles how I became a leader, and more importantly, an authentic leader. As I was coming of age in the '60s, authority was being challenged on many fronts. So when people of my generation were in a position to lead, we were determined not to assert power over people. As teachers, we experimented with "open classrooms," putting much more emphasis on process than on curriculum. As parents, we had a very difficult time saying no, and we wouldn't have dreamed of saying, "Do it because I said so."

In an effort not to be bureaucratic or part of "the establishment," we tried laissez-faire leadership, in which there was validation of just about any point of view and little direction or guidance. To show our respect for people's autonomy, we resisted exercising authority, not realizing that acting on our own authority actually would be the most respectful course of action. When I became a principal in the late '70s, I carried some of these ideas about leadership and authority with me.

It was summer when I first arrived at my school, and the rooms were very dirty. The superintendent sent over a high school student to clean. I tentatively told the student what I wanted him to do, but phrased my direction more like a question. In fact, I ended every request with, "Is that all right?" At one point he shrugged his shoulders and looked away, and it dawned on me that he didn't want to be part of the decision-making process for each little thing I told him to do. He was uncomfortable being directed by someone who was so uncomfortable directing.

Throughout that fall, the students weren't at all sure what to make of a principal who smiled a lot and helped them resolve their conflicts, rather than punishing them, and in some ways I was just as confused as they were. I had been a first-grade teacher and I began my principalship expecting to be a colleague with the teachers—more of a peer, but with different responsibilities.

However, the staff's reaction to me and to my way of leading was largely negative, and my newness contributed to my own uncertainty. I began to believe I would need traits other than the ones I had, in addition to all the competencies I needed to master as a principal. To veil my uncertainty, I thought I needed to present myself as having an assurance that I frankly didn't yet have. I thought I needed to act "as if," until I got there. I sought to become a principal they would respect and value, yet I wasn't sure how to do this. I mistakenly had confused being nonauthoritarian with being authentic, but authenticity does not mean abdicating authority. Additionally, being authentic was even more of a challenge when so many people had expectations about what I should do and be.

I knew who I was as a person, but I needed to learn what it meant to be authentic as a principal. It would not work to define my leadership by the traits other people had used to define their leadership. I would be an authentic leader only if I used the attributes I already had to become the principal I aspired to be. With the help of mentors and other allies, I found the support I needed to once again feel and display the self-confidence I had before becoming a principal. I was moving closer to true authenticity as a leader, which requires claiming the authority of your own experience, claiming your own thoughts and feelings, and sharing them.

In my stories, I describe some of the most painful moments in my career, as well as some of the accomplishments of which I'm most proud. I tell what happened, how I felt, and, sometimes, what sense I have made of it all.

My insights are filtered through my frame of reference, which includes being white and middle class, with all the accompanying advantages of being in the majority. However, as a young, female administrator, I had a profound, though temporary, experience of being the target of prejudice and stereotyping. I gained firsthand knowledge of what it feels like to be a minority. People who have been in the minority for any reason may have experienced some of the same things I did. We often have a lot in common with people who are "nontraditional" in their role. As painful as those experiences were, they opened my eyes, and my passionate commitment to challenging all forms of prejudice was intensified as a result.

Some readers might assume that most women share my opinions, because leaders of minority status are sometimes perceived as representatives of their gender, race, or religion. This perception sometimes prevents people from saying what they think, not wanting to bear the responsibility of being spokespersons. Although I don't purport to represent others' experiences, I do wish to share my own point of view.

I have written these stories with care, wanting to tell them accurately and fairly. Yet I know that other people who were involved may remember and understand them differently. I have chosen not to name the people in my stories, except when given permission to credit writing, music, or artwork, because I want to be sensitive to people's feelings about how they are portrayed to others, even as I articulate my own "truths."

We may all benefit from the knowledge that others have had similar experiences and from hearing how they have dealt with their feelings and resolved their questions and dilemmas. I wish we could sit with a cup of tea and discuss our careers—our aspirations, feelings, and reflections. Because we can't do that, I share these stories as the closest approximation of a conversation that I can offer without being together.

We need to hear more stories about leadership—more voices—from people with diverse life experiences and perspectives. In our own ways, we lead and respond to people and situations. The different choices we make as leaders can inform all of our practices. My hope is that this book will engage you in thinking about your beliefs about leadership and about how you act on them. Please join me in thinking about leadership that is effective, visionary, and authentic.

This is not an important business letter so don't worry . . . I appreciate the way you treat people, kind and caring. And the way everyone's equal. If it weren't for you I don't want to know what this school would be like. You know, it's a stereotype that all principals are mean and that they're all boys. You're definitely a stereotype-buster!

(Letter from Ali McGuirk, age 8,
after a conversation in her class about stereotypes)

CHAPTER 1

A New Person in an Old Role: Multiple Images of a Principal

One time, in search of the principal, a visitor came to the front office. First he looked at the office clerk and asked if he was the principal. When the clerk, a man my age, indicated that he was not, the visitor turned to the secretary. Upon learning that she, a woman older than I, was not the principal, the person at last looked at me. He asked, "Where is the principal?"

First Impressions

"Carl, if you don't get your black butt in that building, I'm going to pick you up and carry you in there!" said Eva, the social worker, to a student in front of the school.

"Well I'm not going," he replied angrily.

Her statement raised all kinds of red flags for me. My mind raced with questions: She's also African American. I'm not. Am I missing something? What did she mean? Why did she say it that way? How did Carl hear it? Unsure, I focused on the power struggle that was definitely unfolding in front of me.

It was the first day of school. I couldn't believe this was happening. Eva's threat to carry Carl inside might have seemed plausible if he had been 5 years old, but Carl was 11 years old and he looked very strong. At this point, my youth and my wish to be taken seriously as a new principal overrode my common sense. I was afraid that my authority was going to be judged by whether I assumed responsibility for Eva's threat, so I took over. When I looked at Eva, I was sure that she didn't expect me to insinuate myself into their conversation. I felt that I was being judged as someone who was too young, too inexperienced, or too scared to death to deal as effectively with this situation as she had.

Carl glared at me, as if to frighten me away, and he will never know how close I came to retreating. I took a deep breath and asked Carl why he didn't want to come into the school, trying to find a peaceful solution to this problem. He wouldn't talk with me and remained adamant that he was not entering. Finally, under what felt to me like Eva's watchful and challenging eyes, I honored her threat and told Carl that if he didn't go into the school by the time I counted to 3, I would carry him in.

Carl was just half a foot shorter than I, and he was much more agile and strong. Yet I picked him up and struggled to get him up the four steps of the entrance and into the school. I think my initial success was because he was so stunned that I actually would pick him up that he didn't completely resist. However, by the time we were in the building and Carl saw that I was serious, he intensified his refusal.

There were eight more steps to get to the corridor, unfortunately complete with a long bannister, which Carl grabbed to keep me from moving us forward. I reached for his fingers, trying to pry them off the bannister while still trying to move his mass and mine up the stairs. For a few moments, it was not at all clear who would win this battle, and I was compelled by the feeling that my whole principalship was riding on my victory. That is probably how I was able to do the impossible: I got Carl up the stairs!

Huffing and puffing, I asked the office clerk to please call Carl's mother. The office clerk, a male, asked if I would like to call her while he held Carl, but after coming this far, there was no way I would let go.

It was probably only a matter of minutes before Carl's mother arrived, but it seemed like an eternity to me. When our eyes met,

I started to explain to her why I was holding Carl with such force, fearful that she might be angry with me for doing so. To my surprise, she had in mind a much more vigorous handling of Carl than I ever would have considered. She glared at Carl and demanded to know why he had acted this way, forcing the principal to carry him in. I thought I detected some respect for my accomplishment in her voice as she interrogated him. Carl cowered in her presence and mumbled an apology to me before promising to be good and go to class. Carl's mother fixed her eyes on me and told me that if I had any more trouble with Carl, I should just come and get her, and she would take care of him.

It was after she left that I had a chance to notice what everyone else in the front office was doing. Everything had come to a standstill as people watched this drama unfold. I wonder if they would have been as surprised if a large male principal had done what I did. They seemed very aware of what I had managed to do, and were perhaps a little frightened, not knowing how out of character this was for me.

As I stood there, I smoothed my clothing and ran my fingers through my hair in an attempt to achieve a look of composure. I felt something very strange happening to my lips. I went to a mirror and saw my lips swelling and turning a bluish purple before my eyes. Evidently I had bitten down on my lips in an effort to haul Carl up the stairs, and now I was wearing a badge of my courage in the form of bruised and swelling lips. Here I was, on the first day of school, and I looked like I had been in a brawl. Things were not working out as I had envisioned.

Larger Than Life

I often wondered if I would ever be widely regarded as the rightful inhabitant of my position. Despite my efforts to establish myself as a caring and collaborative principal, I was continually amazed at how my staff clung to their old expectations of a principal. In the minds of some people, the image of a principal is firmly rooted in stereotypes of age, gender, and style. Because I didn't match some teachers' expectations, they perceived my actions with a more skeptical eye. It seemed that whatever I did or said was always colored by people's projections.

The staff never guessed that loneliness and fear were two of my most frequent companions. I had taken a big risk to become a principal, leaving a school where I was well established as a first-grade teacher, and moving to another state where I didn't know a soul. Rumor had it that I lived with a celebrity, but no one knew who he was because "he traveled incognito!" I was flabbergasted. Another version of the rumor was that I lived with an international airline pilot, but he was often away, so that's why no one saw him. How I wished that either of those rumors were true, when in reality I lived alone and longed for companionship.

Where did those rumors come from? Certainly I didn't create this image, yet people seemed convinced it was true. The belief that I had a glamorous lifestyle with exciting men was some sort of exaggerated fantasy that was flattering and baffling. Although I tried to understand what engendered these assumptions, I wondered if their comments were really about me at all or whether they were about their projections. If only people knew how solitary my after-school time was.

Around that same time, I decided to take up jogging for exercise and stress reduction. I could barely go around the block without being totally winded, but I persisted, jogging each morning with a couple of neighbors before showering and going to work. In a meeting, I reached for a doughnut and one of the teachers exclaimed, "You eat doughnuts?" She asked how I managed to jog 8 miles a day if I ate junk food.

"Eight miles a day!," I exclaimed, "I am working my way up to an eighth of a mile a day. Where did you ever get the idea that I could jog so far?" She didn't know, but she had great difficulty believing me when I said it was not true. In our school, I think that some of the female teachers were not only comparing me with my predecessors, they also were measuring their lives against the life they thought I had and exaggerating the differences.

Children also have had specific ideas about my image and role. Years after I became a principal, a kindergartner noticed a refrigerator in the staff room and asked her teacher, "Is that what Dr. Villani does, buy food for everybody?" Fourteen years older and I had moved from jet-setter and athlete to megamother. Another teacher once told me that she had explained to her class that Dr. Martin Luther King, Jr. was not a medical doctor, he was a doctor of freedom. "Oh, like Dr. Villani," replied an 8-year-old, elevating me to the stature of one of my own heroes.

One commonality of these stories is that they represent me as being "larger than life." The principalship is a job that certainly has many responsibilities with many constituencies. Students, faculty, staff, families, and the community all have needs and expectations that often find their way to the principal's door. Maybe it shouldn't be surprising that there are stories depicting the principal as superhuman. It seems to take someone with extraordinary abilities to do such a job successfully. Some people occasionally might revel in the myth of being perceived as superhuman, but I was very uncomfortable with it because it meant that I wasn't being seen as a real person. No one is superhuman, and any such expectation may result in disappointment, resentment, or anger.

I found that some staff members were continually dissatisfied with much of what I was doing during my first year, yet I had difficulty pinpointing exactly why they were dissatisfied. I later realized their upset was as much about the person I was and what I represented as about what I did. Although they were upset with their new principal, I believe they were even more upset that she could never be like her predecessors, let alone be superhuman. I was an unconventional principal in many ways, and it was very clear that some members of the staff were having great difficulty perceiving me as the principal of our school.

Mirror, Mirror, on the Wall

As I began my first principalship, I heard that a large crowd had stormed a school committee meeting to protest my appointment. One man summed it up this way:

"There are three reasons why she shouldn't be principal. First, she's a first-grade teacher and this is a school for fifth and sixth graders; second, she's 5 foot 4 and weighs 117 pounds; and third, she's a girl!" According to this speaker, only males, preferably large ones, could be effective principals.

I was probably the youngest adult on the school staff and I was nervous. I was eager to show everyone that I was the right choice for the job, so I tried to look the part for a job that didn't typically include young women. Instead of the more colorful suit I wore for the interview, I chose more somber-looking suits to wear to work. Although I understand my reasoning, I feel sorry for the young woman who felt she had to look more like a man. Instead of being excited about beginning my new career as a principal, I chose to deny parts of myself in an effort to be accepted. I was being unauthentic in order to survive and to dispel the predictions of my failure based on the stereotypes held by some members of the community.

Early my first morning on the job, I met a man who had once been the school principal and was still an administrator in the system. He offered to help me place incoming students.

He walked over to the telephone that had once been his and dialed the other principal. "Hello, Mike, this is Sam. I'm in the new little girl's office." I barely heard the rest, being so stunned by both the comment he had made and the fact that he didn't seem to have the slightest idea of how dismissed and invalidated it would make me feel—or did he?

While we waited for Mike to arrive, Sam reflected on his years as principal. He was a tall, muscular man, a former athlete who struck an imposing stance. "Some of the kids here are very tough," he told me. "I used to play a little basketball with them, one on one, you know. And somehow after we played, they got the message and they would straighten out." He looked me over, noting my size, and then added, almost with a note of concern, "I don't know what you're going to do." Neither did I.

A staff member once said, "When Sam was here, it was different. He was like a father to us." I was stung by those words. I remember how my head throbbed. I could never be the father for whom some longed, and I knew I didn't want to be a mother to them either. I couldn't possibly give them what they wanted and still be myself, but could we find a way for them to get enough of what they wanted, while I would retain enough of the person I was?

Finding My Way

I remember the queasy feeling I had in my stomach when I heard Sam's words. He had described a school where physical intimidation was part of the climate, and it scared me. I even wondered, briefly, whether I should register for a karate class.

When I was a junior high school student, I had sympathized with boys who struggled because of the expectation that they show their strength by fighting. I had been glad to be a girl. Now, many years older, I was again facing expectations about using physical aggression to prove strength.

I didn't want to deal with discipline in Sam's way, not because I am a woman, but because it wasn't consistent with my values. I knew I couldn't lead in Sam's way, nor did I want to. I didn't know what my way would be, but I had to find a way that used my own strengths, the strengths I hoped I had.

The staff was confused by my attempts to lead; my approach was new to them. I was confused also; I had expected to be a principal the same way I had been a first-grade teacher, that is, to be authentic, to be myself. Yet it seemed that people had great difficulty accepting me the way I was. To Sam I was "the new little girl." To some teachers I was "larger than life." The more they saw what they expected, the harder I worked to be seen and understood as myself.

Sometimes I felt like I was in one of those carnival mirrors in which the image was so distorted that I just wasn't me anymore. However, we weren't in a carnival. This was real life, in a public school, with children to teach and a community to serve. They needed a real-life principal, not a distorted image of one.

So I became more and more intent on being a leader who was authentic and down-to-earth. Yet to overcome the varied and exaggerated perceptions, I had to put myself even more on display than I typically would in order to correct the misperceptions of the people in our school. People who are nontraditional may find that their differences are hard for others to understand and accept. If misperceptions result, we each must find our own ways to be ourselves, while clarifying the misunderstandings.

I had not intended to be a leader who was so much in the center of things. I had wanted to work alongside colleagues and constituents as part of my leadership. I kept trying to change the focus from supposition about me to the educational goals and challenges of our school. I hoped, at least, that my persistence, as a demonstration of my caring, would convince more of the staff members to join me in doing what was best for the students.

A Little Respect

Changing the focus from me to the needs of our school community was something I had to do in each of my principalships. In another principalship, again I found myself feeling very apprehensive about how I was perceived. At the Lip Sync Shou I was wearing a gold lamé blouse, a tight black skirt, mesh stockings, and lots of makeup. I started to relax when a fifth-grade girl looked me up and down and said, "Gee, Dr. Villani, you should look like this all the time!" A male teacher whom I had hired the previous year was visibly surprised to see me like this and said with some disbelief, "Wow, Susan, you look . . . you look sexy!" It was possible, I assured him.

Although I had had 10 successful years in two principalships behind me, this, my third principalship, challenged me as painfully as when I began my first. When I began my career, I naively expected that if I worked very hard to do the right thing, people would respect me. I was confronted quickly with the reality that effort and good intentions are not enough to do the impossible, which is to please everyone. Although the specifics were different in this principalship, some of the underlying tensions were just as powerful and painful. In fact, it may have been worse. Because I had had 10 years of experience as a principal, I felt ashamed to be in this predicament at this point in my career. Colleagues at my previous school were openly distressed about my departure, yet some of the staff at my new school were up in arms about my arrival. I asked myself, "How could this be happening again?" Dashed expectations and unmet needs are powerful forces in the dynamics of schools at any time. Is it even more dramatic when it is a woman or someone who is not traditionally in the role who is not meeting these needs?

In this school, some teachers and I had worked very hard to build bridges. To create a more positive school community, a "lip sync" show was planned, and students, families, and staff were invited to participate. I chose Aretha Franklin's well-known song, "Respect," for my performance, and several students joined me as backup singers and dancers. Once on stage, I dramatically asserted the song's chorus and its plea for a little respect.

I danced freely to the music, to enhance this plea for respect. I had taken a risk by stating my needs, and what I believed to be the needs of the school community, on stage. At first, the audience was so stunned they were silent, but soon enough they were laughing and whistling. By using humor and music, and portraying a character people could relate to, I had acknowledged a tense situation at school without seeming to be self-pitying or belligerent. By the end of the song, I felt that I had earned some of the respect I so badly needed if I was ever going to be effective in this principalship.

Respect is the cornerstone of mutual relationships. My vision of a school community where collaboration results in heightened understanding and achievement required that all members respect each other. The strong differences of opinion among the staff about my value to them as a principal negatively impacted their relationships with each other, as well as with me.

My sassy statement of the issues in my rendition of Aretha Franklin's song brought the complexities of our plight at school to the surface. Honestly and boldly acknowledging the problems our entire school community faced because there was a question about my efficacy brought us an important step closer to a solution.

CHAPTER 2

Working Through Conflict: Power and Communication

Before we left for our vacation, I had worked up to swimming a mile each day. In Big Tree Calaveras State Park, I couldn't make much progress upriver, as others were doing. I swam as hard as I could, just to maintain my position in the river. I began to doubt my swimming ability, and was later consoled to hear that the altitude often made it harder for people to perform. Earlier in the summer, I had felt relaxed and energized as I stroked through the water and let my thoughts wander. The difference between stretch and stress is significant.

(Excerpted and adapted from the August, 1996, "Welcome Back" letter to the school community)

What Are Our Choices?

In my first principalship, after I physically forced Carl into the building on the first day, it was probably confusing for students to hear me say that they had to work out their differences by "using their words." Students knew that if there was a fight or altercation, they would all wind up sitting in those chairs in my office and talking with each other about their conflict. Over time, they accepted this method. Sometimes I would even be approached by a student with a request to have time in my office with another student, to talk things out.

I became known for this strategy of conflict resolution, although it was incongruent with the way I had conducted myself on opening day. That first day I had done what I thought Eva or Sam would have done, not what I, Susan, would have done under any other circumstances. As administrators, it is crucial that we walk our talk, and I imagine it took me some time to earn my reputation as a caring principal who wouldn't tolerate violence or hurtful behaviors by anyone, including myself.

There were many people in the school community who did not agree with my ideas about discipline. In fact, one parent spoke directly with the superintendent, asking, "Why did you hire her to be the principal, if she won't even hit the kids when they're bad? I told her to just give him a few whacks and he'd behave, and she just won't do it!"

There were several times during my first few months when students also were surprised by the way I helped them solve problems without punishing them. They would tilt their heads in delighted disbelief as they asked, "Are you sure you're the principal?"

One night, during a concert in our school, there was a heated argument between two young men outdoors, near the very steps where Carl and I had faced off on that first day of school. Dick, the evening custodian, had been vocal in the past about his fear that he would have to take responsibility for things that weren't really his job because I wouldn't be able to do them. Sure enough, Dick came to tell me about this fight, muttering about supposing he would have to handle it.

This time I responded differently than I did on that first day, although I was plenty scared. I went outdoors, trying to look taller than my true height. Two older adolescents were yelling at each other, flaunting their bravado. I managed to ask what was happening without my voice audibly reflecting the shaking that was going on inside my body. The crowd had parted when I approached. Clearly people were watching to see what I would do with these high-school-age boys, whom I didn't know. I told them that I couldn't have them fighting outside the school and didn't want them to take their fight elsewhere either because I didn't want anyone to get hurt. "I know I could call the police, but I'd rather not do that," I continued.

With some muttering and posturing, they lowered their voices. I coaxed, "Won't you please come inside and enjoy the concert? It's actually quite good." Once I had gotten them to stop fighting, I reasoned that they might respond better if I invited them in without trying to use the power of my position to get them to act. Had I insisted on their doing what I said, I would have run the risk of creating a new confrontation—with me. By making the choice theirs, I gave them a face-saving way to stop fighting. Sometimes that's all people need to extricate themselves. When people can't see another way, they may feel they have no other choice than to fight.

I must admit to being surprised by how quickly one of the young men responded to my offer to come into the school. Smiling sheepishly, he seemed relieved to have an excuse to avoid the big confrontation that had seemed inevitable only minutes earlier.

As we walked into the school, I couldn't help but glance at Dick, having shown him and everyone else that there was more than one way to deal with a situation. I could use reason. I didn't need to intimidate people physically. Actually, I let my size and gender work to my advantage in this situation. I knew that the young men would not feel physically threatened by me, so they could respond to my invitation without worrying that anyone would think they had been coerced.

There are many ways that a leader could handle this situation, and they all could be successful. What is most important is not the particular strategy I chose, but that it was congruent with my values—it was authentic.

Of course, had both of them been truly invested in fighting and hurting each other, my strategy might not have worked. Then I would have had to resort to calling the police, because this time I obviously would not have been able to carry anyone anywhere. With so many people questioning my capability, times like these were evidence that I could lead effectively, and sometimes I needed to see the evidence as much as they did.

Taking walks with students when they were sent to me for misbehavior was another strategy I developed on the job. As we walked outside, I could see the tension melt from the students' bodies. They talked more freely about their feelings and seemed to be more open to thinking of alternative strategies for future situations. As the anger and frustration of the moment dissipated, and we walked side by side, we could be partners in addressing a problem.

I worked hard to communicate that this principal was strong enough to meet the challenges, but could be gentle and warm as well. The students seemed to be able to accept what I offered more readily than did many of the adults. How to work through conflicts with the staff was an even greater challenge.

Lonely at the Top

Do you remember what it was like in junior high school when some of the really popular kids were planning a party or choosing teams? You'd wait and hope, knowing deep inside that you probably would not be chosen. There was something so tantalizing about being part of this team or group that you desperately wanted to be included. These longings from adolescence resurfaced for me the first year I was a principal.

At times, the staff acted like cliques of adolescents, sanctioning someone who didn't adopt their ways of doing things. I had the feeling that some of the staff members had made a pact to get rid of me. Because I dealt with conflict in a way that was unfamiliar to them, they may have felt the need to take their dissatisfaction underground. However, their anger leaked out through passively hostile behavior.

The year that I arrived, there seemed to be an ever-increasing number of after-school social events among the staff. They would have dinner, go shopping, and take day trips together. Being excluded from these events was not problematic, because I never expected or wished to take part.

Then the teachers started having more social activities at school. The most obvious additions were gourmet lunches during their lunch hour. They brought in tempting delicacies they had prepared at home and heated them in the faculty room toaster ovens. Fantastic smells wafted down the halls of the building and enticed everyone to want some of what smelled so good.

All the adults in the building were invited to attend these fabulous feasts, everyone except me. At first, I couldn't believe that I had been omitted on purpose. I told myself that maybe they had forgotten to invite me in the scurry of all the preparations. When it happened again and again, I knew that I was excluded by design.

This may not have been so unbearable if it had been restricted to lunchtime, but the event literally went on all day, what with the advance preparations, announcements of the menu, smells working their way toward everyone's noses, and then the exclamations of praise and the requests for recipes that followed.

I simply couldn't comprehend that people—that teachers— would be so purposefully hurtful. "They must really hate me to do such a thing," was what kept coming to mind. I tried to tell myself that I was not in junior high and that I needed to rise above their pettiness and remember why it was happening. Yet I felt so distinctly isolated and rejected that this was hard to remember. My mind tried to reassure me, but I still felt the pain of their exclusion.

It is often said that it's lonely at the top. In my case, I didn't feel lonely from being at the top, because they were making me feel like I was at the bottom of the heap, and I was letting them. I tried to reassure myself by focusing on the inappropriateness of their expectations, but I often was overwhelmed by the feeling that my efforts to create a sense of community among such diverse and often antagonistic members of the staff were futile.

It was clear that, to many, my presence was more of an irritant than a unifying catalyst. I was not the principal anyone expected. I was not male, not middle-aged, and not physically imposing. Could a real principal be female, young, and petite—or atypical in other ways—and be accepted? Could I ever be seen as worthy or would I always remain an aberration, maybe even a fraud, in the estimation of others?

It was imperative that I get other perspectives and also that I make other lunch plans. Because I couldn't always get support from outside allies while I was at school, I knew I needed to give it to myself. Between the encouraging words of my allies and my own continuous affirming self-talk, I managed to keep going back to work each day.

In addition to the pain I was experiencing, there were negative consequences for others as well. The staff members were spending a great deal of time and energy planning ways to unnerve me and challenge my leadership. When people's energies are directed toward hurting another, the hostile environment that is created poisons the atmosphere for everyone. Resources squandered on negativity are not available for positive outcomes for students, families, and the staff themselves. I believe we all suffered.

It was probably at about that time that I read this statement: "Our enemies are our greatest opportunity for growth." I remember silently shouting back, "Yeah, if they don't kill you first!" However, the more I thought about enemies presenting chances to grow, the truer it seemed to become. Although it was difficult to sort out at the time, those awful episodes at school were an important part of my development as a leader. I needed to think more about the forces that were driving the teachers to treat me the way they did.

Their fantasies about my lifestyle reflected, and may even have fueled, their impression that I was "larger than life" or better than they were. By orchestrating these luncheons, they had created a way to knock me down to size and reclaim their desired social position. Week after week they made themselves the center of attention, and I was alone.

Although what they did was hurtful, I felt better when I began to see that it was a defense against their own confusion or uncertainty. If they didn't know what to expect at the school since I had become the principal, then at least they could control the guest list for their luncheons. When I grasped how threatened they felt, they seemed much more vulnerable to me, which eased my own defensiveness.

I began to realize that their actions wouldn't have hurt me as much if I had not continued to be so invested in belonging. It is an understandable wish, yet when it became clear that building community would be a long-term project, I had to let go of my immediate yearnings and examine the group dynamics of our school. It is crucial that a leader be able to analyze group interactions and to plan based on these dynamics. My experiences my first year pushed me to learn how to do this more quickly than I might otherwise have done. I became more adept at anticipating people's reactions and strategizing how to approach situations accordingly.

Although I had come to that school anticipating that we would all work together for the good of the students, teachers frequently had discussions about things they didn't want me to hear. Likewise, as a principal, I needed to maintain confidentiality, either to protect personnel or to respect people's wishes to keep private what they told me. Not being able to speak about these things also contributed to my feeling of being removed. Thanks to the training I got in my first year, in what felt to me like boot camp, I have been able to understand the separation that sometimes exists between staff and myself with much less angst.

Over time, I have learned that I can do what I think is right because I don't have to be held hostage by my wish to be liked by the teachers or by my fear of their rejection. Of course I still prefer that people like me, but I know that if I could survive the "gourmet lunch bunch" my first year, I can do what I have to do despite the social pressures staff or parents in the community might exert.

Stuck in Righteousness

In my first principalship, sometimes even the simplest things I had written in memos to the staff were misunderstood and became cause for uproar. I was concerned that misunderstandings were preventing us from building the rapport and trust that I knew were essential to a good working relationship.

My solution, at the time, was to post the memos in the front office of our school. I reasoned that if the teachers read them there, the secretary or I would be able to clarify any misunderstandings on the spot and prevent the permutations that seemed to develop as the memos were discussed in the faculty lounge.

What I didn't understand was that the real issue was new leadership and people's feelings about it, rather than any misunderstanding about the content of the memos. Therefore, searching for a solution about memos would never be the answer.

Just as it seemed that posting the memos had solved the problem I perceived, the situation escalated. The staff wanted copies of all the memos. At first I felt thwarted by their request, because the whole idea was to have the teachers read the memos in the office, where either the secretary or I was present. I began to sense that the teachers wanted copies of the memos to collect "evidence" about me. I refused. After so many other slights, this was the last straw. Unfortunately, I had chosen the wrong time to stand firm and assert myself.

I said that we were a small staff and there was no reason to make copies of these memos. I told them I thought it would be more communal to have a central place where people could read them. However, it was a mistake to refute what they said they needed. To justify their demand, they countered that there were things they were required to do in response to the memos, so they needed copies as reminders. I said that they could take notes from the memo that was posted in the office. We now battled over my refusal to respond to their request for copies. I weakly said that I didn't want to waste paper. Then, when I put little notes on students' lockers asking them to please close their locker doors, the teachers countered that because I used paper to write notes to the students, why wouldn't I copy memos for them? I quickly asserted that I thought there was a difference between children and adults. We were in a battle that never should have happened, but I couldn't see my way out.

A confidant outside of school suggested that I not use memos to share information. Why not have morning meetings to share the contents of the proposed memos and thereby side-step posting or duplicating the information? I implemented this idea immediately, in the hope of extricating myself from this tug-of-war. The way I jumped at this idea reminds me of the boy outside our school who was so ready to accept my invitation to come inside because he really didn't want to fight. I didn't want to fight either, but I felt that my authority was being tested and I had chosen not to back down. I had to learn the hard way that this was not the way to win anything, least of all respect.

I began to have grade-level meetings every few days to talk with teachers about school issues or whatever else required their input, but their response was less than positive. Now, I surely can see their point. They were being coerced to attend these meetings. They and I both knew it. Although they had to come, they couldn't be made to like it or to participate in a dialogue, so it became a monologue, with me talking and them seething.

My inexperience was further exemplified by my indecisiveness about incoming mail. Because I was new, I wasn't sure which mail was important and which could go immediately to the "round file." At these morning meetings, I sometimes would mention something, such as an educational contest, that came in the mail and ask teachers' opinions about whether we should have our students participate. One teacher later characterized these morning meetings as "Susan reading the mail to us." Her words stung, not only because they trivialized my intent for these meetings, but also because there was an element of truth in what she said. An experienced principal would have been able to sort through these offers and decide if any were worth pursuing.

Although I spent a lot of time being angry with the teachers for being so unfair and unresponsive, I realized that if I wanted to be effective I needed to understand them. They clearly were not interested in walking a mile in my moccasins. I would have to walk in theirs. So I took the first step. True leadership can happen only if people are willing to join the leader, and that also requires that the leader do the joining.

I couldn't make the teachers respect me, and my invalidation of their feelings clearly was having the opposite effect. Now I know that articulating my understanding of another's feelings is a much better way to invite a dialogue, even when the conversation may be about differences of opinion. I can try to justify my own feelings and my actions, although what I did was really very silly. It was important to realize that I was getting stuck in a situation I simply could not change. The teachers' behavior in this situation was about my newness. I couldn't rush the process of our getting to know each other, no matter how intolerable I found the teachers' behavior to be.

Sometimes leaders can make a situation feel more bearable by remembering that people's actions often are not as "personal" as they may seem. I wish I had known more about group dynamics when I entered this principalship. Even though I knew a lot about teaching and had worked in a family business for many years, I was not prepared well enough to understand the complex interactions in our school from an administrative perspective. By taking graduate courses in educational administration, I learned about some of the forces that were driving the very things I was experiencing at work. I also had the camaraderie of other administrators, which enabled me to distance myself from the situations and realize that some of the dynamics were predictable, regardless of the individuals involved. These insights helped me grow in my ability to grapple with challenges more objectively, rather than feeling them quite so personally.

For the Sake of the Students

All of a sudden, students were being sent to the front office for disciplinary reasons at a phenomenal rate. At first there were 10 of them, and then the crowd thickened to many more. The reasons the teachers wrote on the office referral notes seemed insignificant, and the students were boisterous and indignant about being sent to see me. What should I do? What would *you* do if 50 kids suddenly appeared in the front office?

I had implemented a system for discipline that required any student sent to the office to complete a form before seeing me. The students had to respond to three questions: What happened? How do you feel about it now? Is there anything else you want to tell me?

The secretary was busy giving out these forms to the students. The office clerk was furiously trying to provide pencils for all the students who needed them; our pencil sharpener had never seen such action. In fact, we had never seen this many people in the front office at one time. It seemed highly implausible that everyone had misbehaved at exactly 2:00 p.m., 1 hour before school was to be dismissed.

I had to spend some time figuring out which of the students were involved in the same incident, so this sorting process used up some of the hour that I had left. I tried to see as many groups of students as possible, but they all left at dismissal time to board their buses, and I was left to make sense of this mess. I stayed at the office and telephoned each student at home to hear what had happened. By 10:00 p.m., I had spoken to every student involved, and felt reasonably sure that none of them had done anything terribly wrong. In fact, I questioned why they had been sent to see me at all.

The next morning I heard what really happened from a staff member who wasn't a teacher. The teachers had agreed they each would send five students to the office at the appointed hour to see how I would handle the situation, and all but one teacher did. At the time, I felt like I had only one ally among all the classroom teachers. Were there no other teachers courageous enough to defy peer pressure? Were there no others who could put the children's needs first? What they did was outrageous. Experience had not prepared me to deal with this situation. Still, I doubt that there are any principals who ever have been faced with this situation, no matter how much experience they have.

I did not confront the teachers with what they had done. If they could use their students to express their own feelings about me as a principal, I was fearful that to engage the teachers would be to further entangle the students in this war-zone mentality in our school. As much as I wanted justice, I felt protective of the students, so I tried to deal with the presenting situation as best I could and move forward.

However, I wasn't allowed to move forward. A few days later, several students came to my office in tears. They said that they were studying democracy and that their teacher had told them the way they could learn more about it was to circulate a petition among the students in the school. The petition said that I was a bad principal and should be fired. These girls were crying because they didn't want to collect signatures from their peers to fulfill their assignment.

I can't believe I didn't confront the teacher about this contemptuous behavior and mockery of democracy. The students were the ones who actually showed the most courage in this situation. After reassuring them that I wouldn't be fired, I once again went about my business. I think I was trying to hide, perhaps from myself, how publicly shamed I felt that a teacher in our school would involve students in a vendetta against me. Such a despicable act certainly revealed a great deal of contempt for me. I tried not to let on to the staff how enraged and vulnerable I felt. I'm sure I also felt paralyzed by the abusiveness of the situation, as well as by my confusion about how things could get to such a fevered pitch.

In the past, when the teachers had summoned union leadership from the state level, I actually had been relieved. I thought that an objective union staff member would help the teachers put things in perspective. Instead, this time he was very cavalier about the events at our school, mocking me and playing to the teachers, who tittered at his comments.

The intimidation and ridicule by the state union representative left me feeling beaten down and gun-shy about confronting the teachers again.

While the teachers went out for drinks together after these episodes, I went home alone. My whole focus at that time revolved around my job. Because I was new to the area, it was taking time to make new friends and establish a local support network. My feelings of isolation made the teachers' strategy at work all the more effective.

So I guess it's not surprising that I simply refused to engage the teacher about the horrifying, mean-spirited behavior regarding the petition. I was afraid that naming it might cause a further downward spiral, yet I knew that ignoring it wasn't right either. As a "good woman" and a "good principal," I was trying to "make nice," remain calm, and find a peaceful settlement. However, there were serious consequences to my choosing such a path.

What still bothers me the most about not handling that situation well is that I didn't attend to the students' needs. I clearly had been intimidated by this scandalous behavior. Students must have had a lot of questions about what was happening, and some of the youngsters clearly were distressed. Putting my head in the sand wasn't going to make their confusion go away. By not directly confronting the issue, I missed an important opportunity. I didn't model strength or courage.

It's hard to have courage in this kind of situation. Addressing the incident of the petition would have been like putting kerosene on a flame. Because I wanted to avoid an explosion, I was reluctant to make that choice. I felt like a hostage in an unstable environment in which there was no mutually agreed-upon code of ethics. The teachers' behavior in these two incidents was so heinous that I sometimes felt like I was working in a crazy place, and, like people in traumatic situations, my sleep was affected greatly. I would wake up literally every hour throughout the night, as if I needed to check my back. That's how frightening I found these school experiences.

I couldn't imagine the teachers doing this to each other. Was their behavior because I was the principal or was it driven by their reaction to my personality or my approach to leadership? Did it have anything to do with my being a woman who was relatively young? They hadn't done this to previous principals, yet they had not had a principal who was nontraditional. I had never encountered this kind of treatment before from colleagues, so I searched for a way to understand it.

Women as Principals

Women are expected to attend to others' needs, and in fact are sometimes criticized when they put their own needs or ideas first. As a result, women often swallow their voices and try to keep the peace. Although I struggled to be perceived as a leader who spoke up, my uncertainty was probably evident. I had temporarily lost my voice.

I'm not sure how I managed to keep persevering in the face of the animosity I experienced, but I was determined not to leave without having had a fair chance to succeed at what I was trying to do.

My thinking about leadership when I began my principalship was much more about the traits necessary to do the job than the characteristics of the individual in it. I've come to understand that the gender of the person in the position has a strong effect on how that person's behaviors are perceived by the different constituencies. In some people's opinion, he is assertive; she's aggressive. He is passionate; she's hysterical. He has idiosyncrasies; she's crazy.

Women aren't the only targets. I believe that every person of minority status has been subjected to perceptions that reflect a double standard. Minorities and people who are atypical in any visible way very often are observed with a more critical eye by some percentage of their constituency. Even if it is a small number of people who are unsupportive in this way, their judgments sting.

For me, the most obvious ways that I was different were gender and age. Many people equate leadership so much with being male that, when asked to list as many leaders as possible in a given amount of time, every group I know of has listed mostly, if not all, men—white men. For many, men remain the leaders and women the caretakers.

Yet even when women are the leaders, do we consciously try to be more like the stereotype of male leaders? Are we less likely to engage with students in childlike play, because of the misperceptions or stereotypes we are trying to overcome? Do we feel compelled to wear dark suits, rather than floral dresses? Do we strive for an institutional feel to our offices rather than making them warm and inviting? We grapple with these issues in our own careers, and as educators we have a responsibility to help students broaden their thinking, both as they view others and as they contemplate their own roles and futures.

Truth or Dare

Throughout my career I have wanted to help students clarify their beliefs and use their voices and their behaviors to assert themselves. An experience I had later in my career was an excellent opportunity for me to do just that. It was 9:00 p.m. when I approached the cabin of my 11 charges for the next two nights, and I did not like what I saw. The girls were gyrating their hips and giggling as they beckoned to the boys in the adjacent cabin. Although the girls were laughing, I knew this was serious. This was about role perceptions and belonging. The girls were inviting a reaction from the boys, but I knew they needed one from me as well.

"Stop," I called to them, but they continued. My middle-aged self was thinking, "I'm getting too old for this." I quickened my pace and kept calling to them, but they kept shaking and waving to the boys. Then I saw Amy doing a shimmy and there was even more shouting and laughing. By this time, I was angry about being ignored, and I walked up behind her and said in a stern voice, "Get in the cabin. All of you." Amy almost jumped out of her skin, and then everyone went inside. After a few minutes, I thought about how uncomfortable the girls, especially Amy, probably were about being spoken to so forcefully. What a way to start off our fifth-grade trip, a trip designed to build self-esteem through risk taking!

I found Amy and said I was sorry that I scared her, but told her of my frustration when she and the others had not responded to my four attempts to get them to stop. "We never heard you," she said, and I realized that the noise they and the boys were making probably had prevented them from hearing me.

"The real reason I was so upset," I told her in a softer voice, "was that I want you to maintain your dignity."

Amy looked puzzled and asked, "What does that mean?"

I was surprised by her question until I thought more about the words I had chosen. I wondered to myself, "These days, does any 11-year-old think about behaving with dignity?" I was starting to feel quite ancient. I knew I had to pursue this because I care deeply about how emerging young women perceive themselves and present themselves to others.

I talked with Amy about how natural it was for girls to be curious about boys and for boys to be curious about girls. I understood that the girls were being a little provocative in a playful way, but I was concerned that some of their movements made me think that the girls were not maintaining respect for themselves. Amy listened carefully to what I said about dignity. Then she apologized. I appreciated that she had heard me and told her I wasn't angry with her. It wasn't a question of fault, and I wasn't looking for an apology.

A few minutes later I decided to speak with the rest of the girls, and they had the same reaction to my statement about dignity. They seemed genuinely interested when they asked, "What do you mean by maintaining our dignity?"

How could I explain this concept without the girls thinking I was referring only to wiggling their hips? I wanted the girls to understand that how they presented themselves mattered in many different situations, not just with boys.

After we talked, another girl, April, asked if I would play "Truth or Dare" with them. I don't know if it was the twinkle in her eye, the raised eyebrow, or the beginning of a smile, but I knew I'd be letting myself in for something. Yet I wanted to balance my initial anger with them by joining in what they wanted to do.

"Truth or Dare," I learned, is a game in which a bottle is spun and when it stops, the person it points to is asked a question or given a dare. I hesitated. To get me to play, April offered the option to "pass" if I really didn't want to respond. Although I don't favor this kind of game, I took a deep breath and cautiously said I would play. After talking about dignity and my values, I wanted to hear what went through their minds.

The first thing April wanted me to do (after she manipulated the bottle so that it pointed to me) was to go up to the lamp and make believe I was dancing with it as if it were a boy. She whispered to friends that she wanted me to dance in a "sexy" way. I'm not sure whether the girls were tittering about her audacity in asking me, about the thought of my being seductive with a lamp—or anyone, for that matter—or out of nervousness about what I might say or do. When I refused to dance seductively with the lamp, April walked right up to me and put her face in mine. Ignoring the fact that she had been the one to assure me I could pass, she taunted me, "Chicken, chicken, what's the matter, are you a chicken?"

Although it was shocking that a student would act this way with the principal of her school, April had a history of being candid, and she knew what she could expect from me, even if she did something that I found unacceptable. Even though I was more than 30 years older than April, and the principal of her school, part of me still felt pressured by her dare.

I asked incredulously, "Do you really think that I will be intimidated by you calling me a chicken? I'm not going to do something I don't want to, just because you are teasing me." After I said that I wouldn't do it, I thought more about April's peers. If it took a bit of strength for me to defy her command, I could only imagine how difficult it would be for her friends. April could be very convincing.

I had several choices about how to respond. I could have been indignant and refused to put up with that kind of behavior, or I could have reminded April that she had offered me the option to pass. Both choices would have side-stepped the real issue and I would have missed a chance to interact meaningfully with the girls. For me, this was an opportunity to model a way to refuse to do something. I could show the girls how setting limits was one way I maintained my dignity, and I hoped to empower them to set their own limits.

"I don't think your friends will always do what you want them to do either," I said to April. My motivation was neither to divide and conquer nor to put April down. Her friends should have a true choice if they were dared to do something. I wanted to add possibilities to their options and to give them permission to do what they really wanted.

I also hoped to give April a chance to learn how to deal with a challenge to her social authority. April had trusted me enough to risk dropping her student-to-principal mask and to speak with me directly. I believe she knew that I would not "pull rank" and hide from her challenge by using my institutional power. She knew that I would show my respect for her regardless of what I said. If there was any power I would call upon, it would be my personal power, which came from my own self-respect and dignity.

April did get some other girls to go up to the lamp, but when they got there, they asked her what they should do. She demonstrated and they tried to imitate her or did their own dance. I wondered, with a bit of worry, what prompted April to do this, but I knew that my immediate response needed to focus on the dynamic among the girls and on dignity and decision making.

Although her voice was tentative, one girl, Jenna, did refuse to do the dance. She looked at me, as if to get confirmation that she didn't have to do it, just as I had chosen not to. By seeing me model assertiveness and communicate my feelings, Jenna was able to state her own refusal. Had I used my age or institutional power as the basis of my response to April, Jenna would not have seen something she could do also.

As quickly as all of this started, it was interrupted when Danielle asked if she could put makeup on me. Perhaps she was getting bored with the whole game and was ready for a change, or was Danielle trying to avoid an inevitable confrontation between April and Jenna about the dare? Did Danielle sense the need to discharge the situation in which April and I held opposite points of view? If I allowed Danielle to put makeup on me, none of the other girls would be in the position of having to choose to comply with or defy April's dare. Instead of being in a situation in which we were at odds, we could all join together. I wondered if Danielle's idea subtly gave more credence to my thinking by making me the center of attention. (Danielle had asked to put makeup on me, not on everyone.)

I could have chosen to bring the girls back to the issue by suggesting we continue playing "Truth or Dare," but sometimes leadership is as much about knowing when to drop something as when to make a lesson out of it. Sometimes "less is more."

Danielle's request to make me up also took me by surprise, although it didn't feel nearly as risky as April's request. I stalled for time by asking, "Do you intend to wear all that when you climb the high ropes tomorrow?" Her friends laughed and told me that she brings makeup with her all the time, just to play with. It is often younger girls who put on makeup just for fun, and I couldn't help but be amused by how these girls were fluctuating between acting both older and younger than their actual ages.

The girls roared with laughter as they fought to put the makeup on me in exaggerated proportions. When they were finished, they decided that I looked quite good and advised me to wear more makeup to school. "Oh you think so, do you?," I responded, and we laughed about whether that was actually advice I would take. I was struck by the fact that I had been talking about maintaining dignity. With that overdone makeup I might not have looked very dignified, but I believe that in this interaction I was every bit the principal I wanted to be. Danielle and her friends were engaging with me by making me look different, yet ironically I was my most authentic during this encounter.

Being made up was a way in which I was willing to have the joke be on me. By laughing together and even letting them take my picture before I washed my face, I signaled that I wouldn't pull rank on them. Because I was feeling comfortable with myself, there was no contradiction between being firm about things that mattered and then being playful at other times. In both cases, I maintained my personal and professional dignity.

The girls responded to my firmness about dignity because they could sense that it was important and that I shared it because I cared about them. I believe some of the girls wanted to learn how to be assertive, so they focused on my example to try it on for size. They wanted to understand beauty, so they experimented with makeup and its effect on my attractiveness. They had to be fairly comfortable with me to do this. Later that night, I told the girls that if they were upset or didn't feel well, I would not mind if they woke me up at any time. They seemed comforted and pleased. I was their mother away from home. When I wanted them to respect themselves and their bodies, they seemed interested in my opinion, although it clearly came from someone of a different generation. Yet when it came to playing with makeup, we could bridge the age difference and giggle together about how I looked. Perhaps that is why I let them do it.

In this interaction, we stepped beyond our roles of student and principal. The girls' spontaneity and candor enhanced my understanding of them. My efforts to hear them and join them, while being myself, were what gave me influence with them, and together we could all explore some of the issues we face as females: assertiveness, attractiveness, dignity, and conviction.

I believe that communication is most effective when there is a sense of mutuality between the people in the relationship. When we are in a dialogue with people with whom we share common interests or concerns, even if we disagree about appropriate courses of action, we are most apt to hear each other.

In my discussion with the girls, I rejected the use of power based on my position or age. Instead, I made a choice to relate to them by finding common ground, thinking they would be more receptive to sharing their thoughts and beliefs with me, and hearing mine.

I had found a way to relate to the girls that worked for us. Another leader may have established mutuality differently. As long as leaders communicate in ways that are congruent with their beliefs and the situation, the interactions are likely to be much more meaningful.

Knowing When

One of the biggest responsibilities I feel as a leader is the impact of what I say and do, both in the moment of the interaction with the person or people involved and in the message it sends to others.

I don't think that the specifics of what I do in different circumstances matter as much as whether I try to understand people's needs and respond to them, and whether I am trusted. When I was with the girls in the cabin, to be most effective I had to be inside the situation, responding as an individual, as well as outside of it, cognizant of the effect of my words and actions as a principal with her students.

I do not always consider this duality, but after years of experience I have learned that if I respond authentically to a situation, it often turns out to be effective for a broader lesson as well. In the struggle about the memos, when I understood that the staff's mistrust of me reflected their fears, I was then able to let go, to get outside the situation, and begin to defuse it. The girls in the cabin knew me and already had decided that I could be trusted. The young men about to have a fight the night of the concert may have taken a chance with me because I showed that I was aware of some of their needs and willing to join them in exploring alternatives. In each situation, I was able to use my influence as a leader because of three things: concern, understanding of needs, and trust. Another person might say and do things differently in any of these situations, and it could be equally meaningful as long as it is genuine.

One of the mistakes of leadership is not knowing when to push and when to let go. When I didn't address the situation about the petition against me, I let something go that I shouldn't have. When I insisted that the memos be posted in the office, I pushed when I should have let go. When Danielle changed the course of events by suggesting she put makeup on me, I think I got the balance right by going with the flow.

When I think of conflict and leadership, I often think of an Eastern way of dealing with force. If a person pushes us and we try to hold our ground, we may fall over. If we take the energy that comes at us and move with it, fluidly, we may maintain our balance. Resisting may feel good for the ego, but it doesn't usually work in the long run. Of course there are circumstances in which a firm refusal is the only appropriate response. Wisely assessing the situation, which may be unfolding very quickly, is what a leader needs to do.

As leaders, we must find ways to maintain the vision of our school community, while dealing with the conflicts that inevitably arise among its members. If we find ourselves directly involved in the conflict, we have to consider our actions, both as participant and as leader of the school. We may need to take a more global view of the impact of the conflict on others and act accordingly.

Sometimes individual needs conflict with the policies or practices of the school community. In those situations, a leader's acknowledgment of the feelings, as well as a restatement of the guiding principles, may be the best course of action.

CHAPTER 3

Being a Leader and Being Myself: Feelings, Attitudes, and Roles

When I was in kindergarten, my teacher thought I was a leader. I clearly remember a statement she made when we were preparing for our graduation ceremony. She appointed me to be the leader of the girls and Warren to be the leader of the boys. Then she said, "Girls, follow Susan. Warren, you follow Susan, too." My teacher confided that she was counting on me to lead the graduation procession and I just couldn't be absent. "People are counting on you." I took this comment very seriously and held onto that message long after I left kindergarten.

Symbols Communicate More Than Style

Symbols are a powerful leadership tool. In my three principalships, I have found that symbols can be used to announce or emphasize important messages to the school community.

When I walked into what was to be my office in my first principalship, I encountered a barricade. The former principal had arranged a large, gray metal desk and two gray filing cabinets in a row, facing the entrance to the office. I knew I couldn't work in such a set-

35

ting, so I decided to tear it down and build one that I thought would be right for all of us in the school community. Although I wasn't sure exactly what would be right, I did know that I wanted an office that was welcoming and warm, and would be comfortable for me and anyone who joined me.

In the spirit of finding a way to make my office reflect my style, I set about to find some wooden furniture, scouring the attics and storage rooms of many of the schools and the administration building. People were confused by my unwillingness to accept their generous offers to order some new metal office furniture.

Eventually I pieced together just what I wanted. I placed a refinished oak desk at a diagonal to the doorway, with a chair to the side of the desk; peering over a desk was not the way I wanted to begin conversations. Then I bought a braided rug on which I put oak chairs in an oval configuration. Floor lamps, braided chair pads, a tapestry, and student artwork added the aesthetic quality I desired.

I had created a warm environment, where the furniture and how it was arranged conveyed an invitation for conversation. Authoritarian power was not the message I wanted people to receive as they entered my office. I was beginning to tell people how I envisioned connecting with the members of our school community.

In another school where I became the principal, youngsters would stand and patiently wait behind a front office counter that was so high that the adults on the other side didn't even know someone was there. When I began that principalship, I had a section of that counter cut out so that it would be evident immediately that a child was on the other side. This work order was one of the most important actions I took as principal in my first year there. It told the community that I valued the kindergartners as much as the sixth graders, and that the physical setup of our school would accommodate the five-year-olds as well as it served the twelve-year-olds and adults.

Desks and counters are not the only things that can keep people apart. I recall when Gina asked me about the coffee fund at the first faculty meeting of one of my new principalships. I was a little bewildered.

I replied, "I don't drink coffee myself, but I'll be happy to contribute if that's the way you do things here."

Because I looked puzzled by her first question, Gina clarified, "How are we going to handle the coffee each day?"

I still didn't get it. "What do you mean?"

"Well," Gina said, "the principal used to set up the arrangements for who would make the coffee and how we would collect the money."

I didn't know whether I was more shocked or amused. "Listen, how you work that out among yourselves is up to you. I don't think I need to have anything to do with that, do you?"

Gina was a congenial person, and she looked at me for a minute to weigh my response. I think it was when she decided I was being forthright that she said a little sheepishly, "This all may seem strange to you, but we are used to the principal telling us how she wants all of these things done."

I knew I didn't have to be in charge of something the teachers easily could do themselves, and changing the protocol was a way to signal that my leadership wouldn't include micromanagement.

Our school logo also told a great deal about how we did things at the third school where I was principal. I had decided that we needed a school logo to put on our stationery and publications, and that the students should be involved in creating it. We decided to have a contest to choose the logo. Our art teacher offered to teach about logos in art classes on every grade level. Design teams of several students each were formed in every class and they worked on entries to the contest.

A panel of adult judges viewed the many logos, which were posted on display boards in the school lobby. Eventually, a logo created by two kindergarten students was selected.

Ironically, some kindergartners initially had objected to participating in the contest because they assumed that adult judges would think that the art of older children was better. However, one of the things that the judges found appealing about the winning entry was that it wasn't overly polished. You could tell that the drawing was done by more than one child; the arms drawn at each end of the row of people were depicted differently. No one pointed this out because no one wanted it to be "corrected." This reflects the philosophy of acceptance and appreciation that the school community had worked to develop and honor. The differences in the picture didn't exclude it as a viable entry; in fact, they made it more charming.

Rather than using some official-looking seal as our logo, we used this picture of three smiling children, symbolizing that children are the core of our school community. We wanted everyone to know that

Figure 3.1. The Thoreau School logo. Created by Will Haver and Meaghan Kilian.

children were our primary focus, and I believe our logo was a constant reminder.

Leaders utilize symbols to convey, simply, what is often the most complex. Visual symbols can be easily understood and remembered, and even can be used to articulate a school philosophy. People must know about the institutions that are significant in their lives, and leaders must use every possible vehicle to communicate their message.

Communicating our message as leaders also includes being aware of how we use our faces and bodies.

"She Smiles Too Much"

My smile has been the source of attention since I was young. In fact, in those early days, I took offense each time someone complimented my smile. There was a reason for my reaction. My younger brother was adorable, and people would stop my mother on the street to comment on his big blue eyes and happy demeanor. After gushing about Paul, they would notice me. The big grins on their faces would start to fade, and they would invariably say something like, "Oh, she's cute too . . . . She has a nice smile." Their expressions convinced me that they were searching for something polite to say about me after fawning over my brother.

"They talk like I'm a horse that has good teeth," I complained to my mother each time it happened.

As I got older, I felt even more uncertain about my appearance. Being an adolescent can be difficult anyway, and having a very appealing younger sibling didn't help my self-confidence. One time when I was moping around the house, my mother advised me, "You ought to smile. Nobody likes to be with a sourpuss." I took her words to heart, especially because at that age I was particularly vulnerable to the thought of not being popular. I smiled more often, and, like whistling in the dark, it became a habit that enabled me to feel more at ease.

Years later, I was startled when someone I had just met at a dinner party asked me if I had worn braces as a child. "What gives you that idea?" I asked incredulously.

"Well, you seem to keep your lips closed when you smile. People often acquire that habit when they wear braces." I was dumbfounded by his observation. After years of being noticed for my smile, now I had been noticed for concealing it.

Thinking about it, I realized that unpleasant experiences at work were probably affecting my smile. I vividly remembered times when I sat in school committee meetings and listened to the newly elected chairperson criticize me for things that had nothing to do with my behavior as a principal. I painfully recalled how aware I was of my appearance as she spoke. Frankly, I didn't know what to do with my face. What she was saying was untrue and vindictive, yet I didn't want to show how hurt I was by her comments. That would have given her more power.

I was being shamed publicly and I imagined people were looking at me to gauge my reaction to her remarks. When people would catch my eye and smile sympathetically, I felt awkward smiling back, yet didn't want to cry either. The compromise I worked out, without much thought at the time, was to smile with my lips closed.

Becoming an administrator opened me to a level of scrutiny that was daunting. It seemed that everything I did was being observed and analyzed. It became clear that I would never please everyone with anything that I did. This seems obvious, yet because I was on the receiving end of the disapproval it was hard for me to take the criticisms in stride. I needed to remember that I couldn't please all of the people all of the time, although the teachers clearly expected me to please each of them.

In one meeting with the superintendent, each teacher came prepared to share a gripe about me. I was most stunned when one teacher hurled the accusation, "She smiles too much." When I told friends about it later, they saw the comment as an example of a teacher lamely searching to find something negative to say about me, and coming up with only this silly judgment. Although I agreed with my friends' assessment, part of me became self-conscious whenever I was aware of smiling.

Being publicly shamed had a deep impact on me. I worked very hard to conceal my pain and found ways to arrange my face that kept people from knowing my true feelings. This worked on some levels, in terms of not revealing how wounded I felt by these unwarranted attacks, but it came with a price. In the process of managing my outward appearance, I was losing track of what was happening for me inside.

Choosing more neutral expressions also denied others the information that might have led some of them to offer me support. There surely have been those who have seen beyond my facade or listened as I spoke with them candidly about how I really felt. Their empathy and support meant a great deal to me, and still does. However, the price I paid for publicly appearing to be unscathed by vicious attacks was that many people never realized how deeply hurt I was and, therefore, could not respond even if they wanted to.

Feeling My Way

Because I was so concerned about the impressions that I was creating with my body language and facial expressions, it was disquieting to have that stranger comment on my smile. His speculation about braces addressed something I didn't even know I was doing. I considered myself to be very self-aware, so his comment was alarming. What else were others able to know about me that I didn't even know about myself? I worried that if I didn't know what I was doing with my face, then I wasn't self-monitoring. If I wasn't aware of what I was doing, I also could miss crucial information about others. These concerns magnified my questions about how I would be perceived.

I was trying to show others that I could do the job for which I was hired, and I didn't want anything I did to reveal my uncertainty or discomfort with any part of my job. I tried to demonstrate my competence, and feared that being too honest about my confusion or ambivalence might create or reinforce the impression that I would not be a good principal, as predicted by those skeptical of my appointment. As a woman, perhaps I was concerned even more about concealing my feelings and reactions at work, not wanting to appear as the stereotypical, overemotional woman.

There is another reason why leaders, both male and female, may consider carefully how much of their own emotional reactions they share with their staff. People may be concerned that we won't be able to oversee events and attend to the staff's or community members' needs while we are feeling and displaying our own emotions. In the face of other people's discomfort, we might decide not to share or process our feelings with the group. We need to resist this option. By being authentic about our feelings, as well as our thoughts, we also may make it feel safer for others to share their feelings or opinions.

Some people need to process feelings in order to participate fully in the agenda items of a meeting. Others want as little processing as possible and find it unbearable when there is anything that interferes with the action items on the agenda. If leaders want to process anything affecting their own emotional responses, there may be even more resentment from those who already have a low tolerance for processing. Making the choice to share their feelings with teachers, if they are feeling unfairly accused or in need of support, may make teachers feel obligated to respond because of leaders' power, even if this is not the leaders' intention. The teachers may perceive that leaders are taking advantage of their role and thwarting the efforts of the group to move forward. Still, it is one of leaders' most challenging tasks to find the balance, on any given day, between a focus on the process and a focus on the outcomes. In addition, the leaders' own feelings certainly affect the process of the group. This must be acknowledged.

We can predict that not everyone will agree with the way we choose to handle whether or when we share our feelings. Modeling acceptance of disagreement about how and what I process in meetings, without being devastated by it, may help other colleagues learn how to handle negative feedback on choices they make. It also actually may free people to disagree constructively without being so concerned that they will anger or hurt the leader that they refrain from speaking.

Group Member, Group Leader

In addition to choices leaders face about the extent to which they share their feelings, they also need to consider the way they share their thoughts. A leader needs to be mindful of not stating an opinion so definitively that it signals that only one point of view is permissible. When the leader expresses an idea, the staff may feel that positional power punctuates the words. If how the opinion is stated implies there is no room for disagreement, colleagues may feel shut down and collaboration will be compromised.

For example, some teachers have very strong opinions about inclusion and their responsibility to meet the needs of every student in their class. In one meeting, teachers heatedly stated that they felt that their skills and hard work were rewarded by having even more students with special needs assigned to them year after year. One teacher, Alex, proposed that all of the children with special needs be put in one room, which would then have a full-time tutor to help teach the children. I responded very quickly that I couldn't live with that arrangement, because I believed it was in the best interests of the children not to be so identified and grouped.

There was mumbling, and glances were exchanged. Although some teachers continued to talk, I later learned from several staff members that many people felt that I had shut Alex down with my comment. They felt this was Susan not listening to what other people think if she doesn't agree with them. I thought a lot about the effect of my stated opinion on conversation and teacher involvement, and discussed this with many teachers over the course of the next few weeks.

There may be many reasons why the teachers wouldn't address this issue with me in the meeting. Some may have feared retribution, and others may have wanted to avoid conflict among colleagues with different viewpoints. Still others simply may not have wanted to prolong the discussion.

Would it have been better to let this suggestion stay on the table, when I knew that it was a suggestion I would not be able to support? I felt that it was fairer to state from the beginning that I couldn't live with it and not let the faculty be misled.

Another time there was a discussion about the effect of tutors entering the classroom to support specific students in various subject areas. Some teachers felt it was disruptive, and they didn't want to have to teach subjects at prearranged times. They wanted the freedom to explore "teaching moments." They valued the flexibility to lengthen a lesson or to integrate different subjects and didn't want to be forced to teach in ways that made less sense to them pedagogically.

One teacher, Pat, went on to say that if what was being done was working for the majority of the children, it wasn't fair to limit a teacher because a few kids couldn't keep up and because support staff were not always available. In fact, Pat wondered if some of the students would be better served by receiving tutoring outside of the classroom, thereby eliminating the need for a teacher to adhere to a prearranged schedule of "in-class" support.

I knew we couldn't sacrifice the needs of any student in order to make it easier to teach the majority. As educators we need to think carefully about all factors and make decisions about what best serves each student, even when it is more difficult for the adults. How could I, as the leader, hold onto this belief and still encourage an open exchange?

I was determined to let people express themselves in the discussion and not to repeat previous behaviors of mine that had shut down conversation. I worked very hard to use body language that encouraged sharing. I was very aware of my facial expression. I tried to convey interest in different points of view. I refrained from reacting to each comment. Instead, I focused on giving different people opportunities to say what they thought. I even asked people whose reactions were evident by their facial expressions to tell us what they were thinking. I purposefully leaned back in my chair, hoping to encourage expression of all viewpoints.

Although I was pleased that people seemed to feel free to say what was on their minds, as they did so, I was feeling uncomfortable. Their thoughts, because they were so vehemently stated and largely unchallenged, appeared to express the majority viewpoint, and I had not voiced my disagreement.

After the meeting, the reactions were mixed. Some said it was a great meeting. Others were deeply upset by what they heard their colleagues say and because I did not challenge the opinions expressed.

I was appreciative that some of the teachers shared their reactions with me. It gave me an opportunity to explain that I had been trying to provide an outlet for their colleagues to express themselves. I told them that I was hoping that colleagues would address each other, rather than wait for me to "come down" on those speaking.

In fact, several teachers agreed that they thought it would be much more effective if teachers spoke with each other. They would rather not leave it to me and then hear the predictable response:

"She's an administrator. Of course she doesn't understand." I later heard that a couple of staff members were specifically advising colleagues to state their thoughts and not leave it to me to say what they were thinking.

I was alarmed that some of our newer teachers, who had not previously heard me speak adamantly about our commitment to inclusion and our responsibilities to all children, felt unsupported or uncertain about where I stood on the issue. As I spoke with the ones who approached me, I urged them to speak with other colleagues if they heard anyone who had concerns similar to their own and to let them know why I allowed the conversation to flow as it did.

I knew that this was an inadequate response. I wish that I had said what I was going to do at the beginning of the meeting. I could have been open about the fact that I wanted to encourage dialogue and, therefore, would not be reacting to each comment. I would have made it clear that my silence did not connote agreement with everything said, but rather a strong desire to let different perspectives be represented.

I imagine some of the staff would have been put off by my saying that I would try not to share my reactions in an effort to promote dialogue. They may not have trusted that I would be open to their opinions because I already had a strong opinion. However, I would hope that some teachers would have remembered times when I changed my mind after listening to their convincing arguments.

Invited Out of the Lunch Box

The first-grade teachers in one school approached me because they didn't want to continue being scheduled for the first lunch period. Early lunch curtailed morning work time and made for a much longer afternoon, when the students' endurance was waning. Teachers also found that the youngsters weren't even hungry at their assigned lunchtime because their morning recess and snack had ended only an hour earlier.

I told the first-grade teachers that I was unwilling to change the lunch schedule on my own. I would be willing to put the issue on a faculty meeting agenda if they were ready to state their case. However, they were reluctant, and for a couple of years they lived with the schedule as it was, rather than addressing it at a meeting with their colleagues. When the first-grade teachers spoke with me again about their dissatisfaction with the lunch schedule, they were prepared to address this issue with their colleagues.

Changing the lunch schedule would have ramifications for specialist schedules, including art, music, and physical education. All classroom teachers were very invested in having schedules that they perceived to be optimal for their students. I put discussion of the lunch schedule on the agenda for the upcoming faculty meeting. We all anticipated that it would be a heated discussion, and our prediction was correct.

One upper-grade teacher remarked early in the meeting, "Over my dead body will we have early lunch. It would mean changing our whole schedule."

"I hope it doesn't come to that, but we are going to discuss it," I replied, trying to inject a note of levity into the meeting, which was becoming very tense.

Evidently no one wanted first lunch, and it looked like we might come to blows—verbally, that is—about who would be the unlucky ones. The people who knew that I had been a first-grade teacher prior to becoming a principal probably would have bet that I would decide in favor of the needs of first-grade students. Yet I respected all of the teachers' advocacy for their classes and sought a way to capitalize on their investments in their students' needs.

We tried and tried, but we couldn't figure out how to fit all our students into the cafeteria in any other configuration than three lunch periods. Some classes had to go to early lunch. Tess, a first-grade teacher, said that she would be willing to have children eat in her classroom rather than have to eat so early in the cafeteria. This was the first solution that didn't just focus on lunchtimes, but rather on where lunches could be eaten.

Louise adamantly objected to having children eat in the classroom because of potential spills on the carpet and food smells for the rest of the day. There was also the issue of how to supervise children during lunch if they ate in individual classrooms. The teachers' contract guaranteed a duty-free lunch to teachers, and we had only a few "noon aides" to supervise the children in the cafeteria. If the children went to separate classrooms, we wouldn't have enough people to go around, and there was no additional money for supervision in the budget. With classroom hygiene and the teachers' contract as objections, it again seemed that there were too many obstacles for us to solve this problem to everyone's satisfaction.

Yet the problems now being aired were administrative issues. I believed that we had to deal with whatever got in the way of doing what was in the best interests of the children. Not solving a problem that affected children's learning was not an option. We had to persevere.

"There must be something we can come up with," I said, more as a question in my mind than the definitive statement I appeared to be making. "It seems a shame for some of our students to be disadvantaged because of a scheduling problem." I let silence have its effect. "What else could we do?" I pleaded, searching for a solution that was elusive.

I was appealing to the dedicated impulses of the staff. They could see that I was open to considering any solution. It was a prime time for the faculty to take a risk, because we seemed very close to defeat otherwise.

"I'd be willing to eat lunch with my own students," offered Tess, desperate not to get stuck with first lunch again. Her comment marked another turning point in the meeting. By stepping outside another box, Tess enabled others to think more creatively and kept the problem-solving discussion alive.

There was heated debate about setting a precedent if a teacher supervised her or his own students in a classroom during lunchtime. There also were concerns about how Jamie, the custodian, would feel when children carried trays of food through the hallways and into their classrooms. We clearly weren't out of the woods yet.

Seth wondered aloud, "What if we found another place for the children to eat so that they wouldn't be in their classrooms? Would that work?" Here was another teacher's attempt to stretch our thinking to new places, both literally and figuratively. I was excited and intrigued by people's creative alternatives.

Rather than a "Yeah, but" response, I wanted to maintain the momentum and convey the spirit of, "Wow, how would we make that work?" I responded that we definitely could think of different eating places, as long as we could figure out how to provide adequate supervision. So the teachers wouldn't be inhibited by a contractual concern, I also reassured them that we could state in advance that anything we tried would not be binding for future contracts.

Before we knew what was happening, teachers started volunteering to take turns doing lunch duty, if only we could find a place. We talked about kids eating in the hallway, but that didn't seem safe. Then Jean asked, "What about the gym?"

There were no physical education classes scheduled from noon until 1:00, so that space was available. We identified the potential obstacles to this suggestion, including food spills ruining the gym floor and the need for more tables and chairs. It seemed that we were onto something, but there were still problems to iron out. The staff agreed to talk to their colleagues about the ramifications of this proposal.

Share the Problem and Invest in the Solution

The dynamics of solving the problem had completely changed. Now we were working together to make a solution work, rather than being divided about whether to tackle the subject. People really wanted to figure this thing out.

There were many conversations among the staff over the next few days. Teachers agreed to take turns supervising the overflow group of students in the gym, and sought Jamie's opinion. They explained the problem to her and described how everyone had joined to make it possible.

Jamie was understandably concerned about how to keep the floor clean, especially with youngsters scheduled for physical education right after lunch. She also pointed out that it would take a long time to move tables and chairs in and out of the gym. In addition, there was the problem of where to store the cafeteria tables and chairs when they were not in use. What seemed to be a big obstacle to others was one that I, as the principal, could solve. I offered to find folding tables with attached benches, as well as the funds to purchase them.

Jamie agreed to be part of the proposed solution. It meant additional work for her, because now she'd have to set up and take down tables and clean the gym floor in addition to her work in the cafeterias. Yet she was willing to help the staff achieve their goal of only two lunch periods. The staff now had the immense satisfaction of solving together what had been a very troublesome problem.

I had been willing to address the issues at a faculty meeting if the first-grade teachers were willing to state their problem to their colleagues. I believed that when they were ready to own it and state their case, they would be more likely to invest themselves in enlisting help to find a solution that would address everyone's concerns. The problem also would seem more compelling to colleagues if they heard it directly from the first-grade teachers. I wasn't going to be the person who would choose a schedule and force people to live with it. Even if I simply had been the one to present the issue to the faculty, it may very well have been seen as "Susan's problem with the lunch schedule." The staff was much more invested in solving a problem that affected their first-grade colleagues than they might have been in rectifying a scheduling problem presented by the principal.

There also were contractual issues involved. I would not have imposed lunch duty on people who were entitled to free time. Because the idea came from the group and the solution seemed the only way to remedy the problem, it was agreeable to the faculty. The teachers, invested in the outcome of this decision, were creative and cooperative about finding a solution and making it work.

As valuable as it is to find a solution to a presenting problem, it is just as important to recognize the importance of problem-solving and decision-making processes. It is often the leader's role to facilitate joint problem solving; it is equally important that the leader highlight what actually happened. In this way, the members of the school community can look back on their behaviors and see the ways in which their collaborations achieved the goal. They also can reflect on what parts of their interactions helped or hindered reaching the goal. Even if we ultimately had concluded that nothing would satisfy everyone's needs, at least we would have worked together to try to solve the problem. People may have become more empathic to the dilemma faced by the first-grade teachers, and perhaps the upper-grade teachers would have been more open to taking turns with the first lunch period or to finding some other compromise.

Our community was learning to take care of itself. Through the course of this meeting, my role as a leader was less obvious, because I provided modeling, momentum, hopefulness, and concern for relationships rather than direction or dismissal of the problem. Sometimes it's most effective for leaders to let the group's process unfold in its own way.

CHAPTER 4

What We Have to Offer: Fitting a School Together

In recognition of all the advice, aid, help, assistance, hand-holding, lesson plans, materials, humor, goodwill, mentoring, butt-covering, chicken soup, advocacy, support, flowers, gifts, smiles, rescuing, collegiality, direction, camaraderie, confidence, and friendship, we, the second-year teachers, thank you!

(Certificate of Appreciation, presented to the faculty
by second-year teachers, Fall, 1996)

Building the School With People

When leaders are clear with the staff and students' families about their roles in the mutual goal of promoting students' growth and achievement, energies are used constructively. A leader's responsibility to foster community includes attending to each constituency, both individually and as they interact with other constituencies. To be attuned to the members of a school community, leaders need to communicate effectively. In addition, leaders need to know themselves, share themselves, and carefully consider their relationships

49

with students, families, and staff. The contributions and interactions of each of these constituencies are what make a school dynamic.

Bringing talented, creative, collaborative, and diverse risk-takers into a school to join existing talented staff is one of the most important things a principal and/or an administrative team does. Parents are sometimes skeptical of new teachers, fearing their inexperience will mean they are insufficiently knowledgeable or skillful. Parents may be concerned about whether new staff members share their values. When I earned a reputation for hiring exceptional teachers, it helped parents trust that the new teachers would be positive additions to our school and good for their children.

I recall one year that was particularly challenging with regard to staffing. Due to a retirement, leave of absence, voluntary transfer, and increased enrollment, I was in the enviable position of being able to hire five teachers. Some of my administrator colleagues felt sorry for me because each new hire required five formal observations and write-ups, and an evaluative summary. They feared the paperwork might do me in. I said that I would rather go down that way, if it came to it, than not have the opportunity to bring in exciting and talented teachers.

I interviewed more than 75 people for those positions, after screening countless résumés and conferring with the Director of Personnel. It was a very time-consuming process, yet it was worth every minute. I met incredible people and recommended we hire a most diverse group of men and women of different ages and ethnicities. I believe it is important for children to interact with people who share their backgrounds (i.e., race, ethnicity, religion, gender). Because teachers are often role models for children, it is imperative that the faculty be diverse. We were hiring talented teachers who would bring new perspectives and capabilities to the entire school community, not just their own classrooms.

An example of how a newly hired teacher shared her talent with our entire school community, while making a strong statement about the values of our school, was when our music teacher wrote our school song. She conferred with colleagues to get ideas about the type of music that would be most welcomed, as well as lyrics that would be meaningful for the children and the adults in our school. Her creation was a triumph. We proudly sing it at school events. The music and words reinforce our beliefs, our sense of belonging, and our commitment to each other.

Figure 4.1. The Thoreau School Song. Composed by Susan Tuttle.

I didn't want there to be divisions among colleagues based on whether or not I had hired them. I made sure to speak about the contribution new members could make to an already strong and experienced staff. To my relief, veteran staff readily accepted these individuals, realizing their value and respecting them. Parents carefully watched these new teachers as well and made their own assessments. The teachers were excellent, and my reputation for hiring was being formed.

Now, teachers that I recommend for hire have the advantage of positive anticipation by many parents, who, for the most part, have strongly approved of the people hired since I came. When a school community anticipates that new staff will strengthen the school and be good for the children, it makes an enormous difference in the likelihood of success for the people hired. As teachers new to our school become oriented to working in a new environment, they are given the benefit of time to show what they can do, rather than being judged on their teaching the minute they walk in the door. Just as children need to feel safe to learn, adults are able to do their best when they feel safe.

Matching the Teachers and the Students ... and Their Parents

One of the first things that parents in every school system discuss with me is how their children will be assigned to classroom teachers. Because parents care so much about their children, it is not surprising that many of them are very concerned that their children get "the best" teacher each year. Yet what does it mean to be the best, and how does one know who is the best teacher at each grade level? Is there really a "best?"

Parents formulate opinions about teachers in many ways. The experience of an older child in that teacher's class is one way; observations during chance encounters in school is another. Neighbors are a big source of information, and opinions about "the best" teachers are often shared.

As teachers develop reputations in the community, parents begin to refer to the teacher who is "good at self-esteem building" as if that description applied to only one person. It is sometimes amusing to hear different parents express the same needs for their children and then name different teachers as the only ones who can meet their needs. Obviously, many teachers can do what is requested, yet parents may know of only one of them by reputation or direct experience. I have worked hard to help people understand that there is not one "best" teacher; rather there are teachers who have different skills that may serve students in different ways.

In addition to teacher–student matches, it is very important to consider the mix of students in each class, because peer interactions can greatly affect student behavior and achievement. A simple sign-up process for classes, as some parents have suggested, would not ensure the needed academic, physical, and social balance. Whereas specific teachers may be especially talented in certain ways, the children need to be equally divided into different classrooms because too many children of similar needs in one room will make it difficult for any teacher to serve the needs of all of the children in the class. Parents don't have this information, and some may have only their own child's needs in mind. However, the school has a responsibility to meet the needs of all of the children.

Although some parents are very trusting of what the school personnel will do, others want to have a more active role in the process, wanting to pick their child's teacher or even select the peers with whom their child best relates. I encourage parent involvement, but placement cannot be decided solely on the basis of parents' preferences. It also would not be fair for the parents who are the most outspoken or who know the principal the best to get what they want—and for the preferences of the rest of the parents to be ignored.

Through the years, the staff and I have developed the following placement process. I mail a letter to all families each March, outlining the placement process used at our school. It explains that there is a core placement team composed of individuals who have responsibilities with children in all the grades of the school. These people are the instructional specialists, social worker, psychologist, speech and language therapists, and the principal. In addition, the teachers of the sending grade level join the team to help place their students in the next grade's classes.

Parents are invited to fill out a form that indicates their view of their child's strengths, challenges, and needs. In this way, they can state what they think has worked well for their child in the past and what they hope for in the future. For many parents, this form is a comfortable vehicle for sharing their thoughts with the school.

In my letter to families, I also include an invitation for them to have a brief conference with me to share any special concerns. As the letter explains, they can speak about what they are experts in—their children. I tell people that I don't expect everyone to feel the need for such meetings, and that many very caring and concerned parents do not meet with me.

When parents do wish to meet, I ask to hear their views on what is optimal for their children in terms of teaching methods and classroom protocol. For example, some families have strong beliefs about the value to students of readily observable structure and discipline. They prefer a classroom in which the primary interactions are between the students and the teacher. They prefer to see less movement around the room and less interaction among the students during class time.

Other families look closely to see if the classroom has opportunities for creative expression through a variety of media. They like to see students working together in small groups and being animated and vocal in their interactions with each other. All of these families want their children to learn. However, they have very different ideas about what best promotes learning.

Many parents appreciate the invitation to speak directly with me about their concerns. I make it clear to parents that the conference is a time to tell the principal what type of teacher and class they want for their child, not which teacher or class they want. I discourage parents from telling me which teacher they think best does what they want and should, therefore, be their child's teacher the next year. Parents might be surprised to hear how vulnerable teachers feel to the conversations about them that, we are told, occur during neighborhood sports practices and local events. Because these conversations are held publicly, teachers are concerned that they may be judged harshly by anyone present based on incomplete, if not erroneous, information. In our meetings, some parents try to "work the system" by alluding to traits of a specific teacher that make their preferences clear, such as "My child is very creative, so he should have a teacher who does drama." Even without a name, if there is only one teacher at the grade level who puts on student plays, the identity is clear. By insisting that parents follow the guidelines for parental input in our placement process, teachers may feel more assured that unfair judgments about them are not determining class placement.

Different assumptions about what influences me are reflected in the ways people choose to approach me. If a father who is not usually involved in communication with the school about his child accompanies his wife to a placement conference and does all the talking, I may speculate that his presence is intended to convey more authority or clout than hers alone. In these moments, I wonder if what I've stood for and modeled about gender equity has been clear. Don't they recognize my great respect for children's mothers? I feel disheartened by any assumption that a father's wishes or demands should count more than a mother's. Then I remind myself that these parents are merely trying to do whatever they think will work to their child's advantage. Being a parent myself, I can identify with parents' motivations even when I disagree with the ways they may act on them.

I have never heard of another principal who routinely invites parents to meet to discuss placement. Some years I have had as many as 100 such placement conferences, which take up the better part of several weeks and are emotionally taxing as well. Many of my administrator colleagues think that this practice of inviting parents to conference with me is not merely time consuming, but is sheer lunacy—especially because I make it clear that I won't promise to give parents the teacher they want for their child. The majority of parents seem to appreciate the time it takes me to meet with everyone who accepts my invitation, and they value their inclusion. However, because they don't get to choose the teacher, some parents still feel shut out of the placement process no matter how much I invite their input.

One year I was so exasperated that I said to our secretary, "If I ever offer to do this again, shoot me." The following year, as I was sending out the letters to parents about placement, including the offer to meet with me, she sheepishly asked me if I remembered what I had said. Luckily, she is a pacifist.

In spite of the inevitable aggravation, I would much rather put in the time proactively than hear from dissatisfied parents after the placement decisions have been made. Our placement process has greatly reduced the number of requests for changes, and some parents who have disagreed with our placement decisions have later acknowledged that the placement team's decision was right after all. Even with all the time invested and all the drama, I still believe our process best serves the students.

Protecting Relationships

As diverse as parents' perceptions about teachers are, the perceptions that teachers have of each other are equally varied. Teachers often know very little about how their colleagues teach because they are usually in their own classrooms teaching. Teachers rarely observe each other, although I encourage them to do so. As a result, they may make judgments about one another's teaching based on their interactions outside of the classroom. They also may be influenced by what former students and students' parents have told them. Despite the fact that teachers lack full information about other teachers, it is very important for them to have input into deciding where their current students are placed for the next year.

At one school, in my first year as principal, I was bombarded with criticisms about a specific teacher. As soon as I arrived at that school, many parents made very disparaging remarks about her. Several went so far as to say that unless I gave them assurances that their children would not be placed in her classroom the following year, they would begin making arrangements to send them to private school in September.

Because I was new to the school, I didn't know whether their concerns were legitimate or the result of incorrect information or unfair conclusions. Without knowing the history, I was not in a position to take as firm a stand against the threats as I would have, had I felt certain the allegations were unsubstantiated.

Either way, I didn't believe that the parents' insistence was information the entire staff should know about, so I decided to change the placement process to protect the teacher's privacy. Placement would be done by a core team consisting of the social worker, language arts specialist, learning disabilities specialist, and speech and language therapist. Sending teachers would write recommendations about placement that would be strongly considered, but these teachers would not sit with the placement team.

Some teachers felt very hurt that they were excluded from the process, and others were furious. At the time, I felt that I could not reveal my reason without creating curiosity about the identity of the teacher involved. Although I tried to allude subtly to the dangers to teachers of picking classes for one another, many teachers concluded that I was devaluing their input.

It was a mess. By the time it was over, I had alienated just about everyone. To top it all off, the teacher I had worked so hard to protect wound up being angry with me about another matter, and she very adamantly told her colleagues that I had not supported her when she needed it! For many years afterward, this teacher would not speak to me, and her behavior embarrassed me. At times I wondered why I had even bothered to change the placement process to protect her when this was the way it turned out.

I know why I did it. It wasn't just for her. I did it because I believe that whenever someone is humiliated among peers it has a detrimental effect on everyone involved. People feel mixed emotions that are difficult to sort out. Most likely they will feel sorry for the person who has been embarrassed. They may be angry with the person whom they believe to be causing the situation or the person making it public. They may be worried that such a thing could happen to them. Sometimes it can be even more confusing for them when they actually see the other point of view but feel disloyal for even thinking about anything other than full support for their colleague. Such situations always have an impact on the morale of the group.

Neither the individual teacher identified by the parents nor her colleagues ever knew what motivated me to change the process. There were extenuating circumstances that I simply would not share with the group. Sometimes principals have to make difficult decisions that people just won't be able to understand. I have found it to be very painful when I've felt misunderstood and judged and I couldn't defend myself by explaining my rationale.

In retrospect, perhaps telling the staff in advance about the situation we faced, without identifying the teacher's grade level, would have helped them understand my motivation for seeking another way to do placement. Instead of feeling shut out, people then could have joined me in finding a better way.

Revealing the Obvious

These days, no one is calling me "the new little girl," but I have noticed that I am still, after all these years, sometimes uncertain about smiling fully in ambiguous situations. Painful past experiences can affect us for many years. The misperceptions about my smile have stayed with me longer than I would have thought, and it wasn't only the perception of my smile that concerned me. When I was just starting my career, the last thing I ever wanted anyone to see was when my eyes filled with tears. Now I don't worry about it as much. Having been a principal for 20 years affords me the choice to share my feelings with people without being concerned that they will think I can't do the job.

Recently, I was interviewing candidates for a teaching position at our school. One candidate told me about two of her brothers, both of whom had died, and about the effect those experiences had on her as a sister and as an aspiring teacher. My eyes filled with tears as she spoke. When she noticed my tears, she stopped talking. She hadn't anticipated anything like this when she was preparing to go to interviews.

I told her that I was deeply moved by her story and that it showed on my face. When she saw that I was comfortable with my own spontaneous reaction, she accepted what I said and the interview continued. When she wrote to thank me for the interview, she included something like, "You are the first person who has interviewed me that responded so strongly to what I said about my family. You must be a very sensitive principal, and I would love to work in your school."

At my age, I have become comfortable with the fact that I am a passionate person. I laugh easily and I cry easily. To my knowledge, it hasn't interfered with my work. In fact, I believe that my passion enhances my effectiveness. If I were to lead in ways that were not authentic for me, they simply wouldn't ring true. People can see that sharing more of myself comes from a deep belief that being authentic makes me a more effective leader.

As people have worked with me or seen me operate as a principal, the reactions have, of course, been mixed. Perhaps it is the trust that has been earned by being more real, more human, and more open that has encouraged people to take risks with me.

It takes courage to be authentic. Sharing one's thinking and feelings, during as well as after an event, can make one vulnerable. To discuss things while they are happening is much more difficult because the context keeps changing and the outcomes are unpredictable. For me, to decide to take risks depends on what I think might be gained. The risks of such authenticity are greater, but so are the rewards.

The process of becoming self-aware and authentic is unending. I continue to learn as I interact with others. By seeing how I have behaved in different situations, people know that I readily change my mind when I am influenced by their perspectives and ideas. Being transparent enough to reveal and identify when this is happening strengthens people's assurance that I will really listen to what they are saying, that it does make a difference, and that I sometimes will change my behavior as a result.

I do believe that aspects of authentic leadership are more subtle than aspects of other approaches, and they may require a longer time to be understood. Focusing on process and relationship takes more time than decision making from above, and the staff initially may have viewed me as being less decisive and less able to achieve results. As we worked together and as I clarified my approach, people have come to understand my leadership and trust it.

Being authentic also includes being spontaneous, so although some things such as a decision-making process may be described in advance, other things will happen as a function of the situations and the people involved. People who value alternative ways of leading are usually more appreciative of my efforts to be transparent about my thoughts and feelings.

When I think back to the young woman, newly appointed, who worked so hard to look like a principal by wearing gray, brown, or blue suits, I see how much difference 20 years makes. I now know more about who I am on the inside and I feel freer to be authentic on the outside. Later on in my first principalship I knew that I had taken a big step when I dared to wear a pink blazer on a television program about our school. Years after that, when I started wearing floral dresses in addition to suits, I had taken another symbolic and authentic step toward sharing who I am without apology.

Even when I haven't made the conscious choice to reveal some part of myself, some people—often children—can see it anyway. One day, when I was observing an art teacher with a first-grade class, Charlie sauntered over to me.

He asked, "Are you Dr. Villani? You look a little different."

I had just gotten a haircut that people were complimenting me on, and I asked if he thought that might be it.

"Yeah, but you also look different in your face," he replied.

"What looks different in my face?"

"It looks a little more wrinkly."

You might think I would have felt very deflated or angry about what Charlie said, but those weren't my reactions. I was curious. I said, "When you wave to me from the hall and I'm sitting at my desk, you're further away from me. Maybe you're closer to me now and can see the wrinkles better."

Charlie backed up to approximate the distance at which he usually sees me, peered at me for a while, with his thumb and forefinger framing his chin, and then concluded that I definitely had more wrinkles than when he saw me last week.

"Do you think I got these wrinkles during one week?" I asked.

"Maybe during the weekend."

I had indeed had a very troubling weekend, and what this little guy had observed was probably the tension I still carried in my face. Charlie's perceptiveness astounded me. Sometimes I am still more transparent than I realize. When I told some colleagues about my conversation with Charlie, they were horrified, but I was smiling.

If an adult had made a similar statement, I would have wondered if criticism and judgment were implied. However, Charlie was merely reporting what he observed, as casually as he would describe any detail he noticed. It felt good to be seen without being scrutinized.

There's a plaque in my home that says, "Wrinkles merely indicate where smiles have been." My face reflects the smiles, the frowns, and all of the experiences of my life. At this point in my career, I am much more comfortable with that reality. Coincidentally, there is a sign on our art room door that says "Be yourself. Accept others."

In the day-to-day functioning of a school, leaders spend nearly all of their time supporting and facilitating the growth of the children and the adults in the school community. It is imperative that we also reflect on ourselves and our own development; when we do so, we become better leaders and we model appropriate self-care to our colleagues.

CHAPTER 5

Promoting Acceptance in the School Community: Each Person's Right to Belong

One day I was having lunch with a first-grader in my office. She was making conversation, asking me if I had enjoyed the weekend, what was my favorite color, where did I live, and if I had children. When she started to run out of questions she asked, "How old are you?" When I told her that I was 42, she asked, "Oh God, how did that happen?" I've been asking myself that same question. After years of being the youngest staff member or the youngest principal, I was startled by her horror at my age.

First Friends

I invite parents to bring their children in to meet me as soon as they know they will attend our school. We sit in my office and I acknowledge some of the things they might think about as new students in our school. "What are the kids like? Will I have any friends? Where's the bathroom? What will my teacher be like? Is the work hard?"

I tell them, "I want to be one of your first friends to start with. If you have a problem, besides your teacher and the nurse and the social worker, I also would be happy to listen. Maybe I could help. I like to hear good news, too, and if you ever want to give me some art or writing you've done, I love to decorate my office with student work."

After answering any questions they have, we go on a tour of the building. As we're walking, I am able to begin to get to know them. Because we already have covered the pressing questions they have about the school, we can chat as we walk, and their personalities show more readily because they are more relaxed.

When I have anticipated children's arrival, I'll bring them into the class they will be in and introduce them to their teacher and students. Then, with my hand on their shoulder, I say to the class, "How would you feel if you were coming to a new school and the principal just started giving you a tour of the building? She's got her hand on your shoulder and you're wondering what she's going to do or say next. How would you feel if you didn't know the teachers, the kids, or if there was going to be recess? Well, I don't know for sure, but maybe Les is feeling some of these things. Who can tell Les something about our school?"

The children say they like recess, the teachers are really nice, and we have special events like the "Turkey Trot" and the "Lip Sync." Then I ask, "Would you please raise your hand if you'll be a buddy for Les? Who will show him (or her) around when he (or she) gets here. Who will eat lunch with him (or her)?" Many hands are quickly raised and the tension in the new student's shoulders starts to dissipate. Within 10 minutes, the new pupils have more offers of friendship than they know what to do with. As we walk back to my office, they are usually much more relaxed.

Knowing what to anticipate goes a long way toward reducing anxiety about being new to a school. Now the new students can focus on our school with anticipation rather than fear. It usually goes very well after that because the teachers take over, and they are masters at helping kids join their classroom communities.

"Just Because"

I believe that what informs the practice of many teachers and administrators is their experiences at home and in school as learners. Although we continue to learn about our profession by studying educational theories and collaborating with colleagues, formative childhood experiences often ground our beliefs.

I'm sure that I pay particular attention to students' entry to our school because of some of my feelings of insecurity when I was a youngster, and even because of my confusion about what being a youngster meant. As a capable and perceptive child, I was noted for accomplishments and behavior seemingly beyond my years. My parents seemed so delighted with my achievements that I wanted to keep improving on my last accomplishment, and I aspired to act older because I thought it was more desirable.

High-achieving students often receive a lot of attention for their accomplishments. They may think that their acceptance is based on their performance and feel compelled to repeat or better themselves to continue being accepted. I, like other high-achieving students, confused competence with acceptance and, furthermore, based my self-acceptance on the approval or admiration of others.

I remember, as a young girl, wanting to wear my skirts at knee length like my mother and refusing to wear them as short as other girls my age. I wouldn't accept lollipops at the doctor's office and refused to go on the rides at the amusement park. My parents took my brother and me there to enjoy ourselves, but I hated going. It wasn't clear to me then, but in retrospect I think I found it confusing to be at a park where I was expected to act like a child, when at other times I was praised for being adultlike. However, for all my yearning to be seen as mature, I surely had the developmental needs of any child my age to feel safe and accepted.

I know I took this wish to achieve and be recognized further than my parents wished. There was the time when my mother offered me the treat of my choice—my first lipstick—if I would just do something that came naturally to most kids. What was so difficult for me to do that she felt she needed to bribe me to do it? To go outside and play after school, and not spend every afternoon redoing homework until it was perfect. It was obvious to my parents that my concern about doing things perfectly was not serving me well. They clearly wanted me to have more balance in my days and more childlike experiences.

My teacher also expressed concern about me. She knew about the bargain my mother had made with me and proposed something new to me as well. She wanted me to work on homework for only an hour each day, and promised that she wouldn't punish me if I didn't finish everything. The day after we made this arrangement, the teacher was reviewing the spelling words with the class. When she called on me to say whether I would wear a b-o-w or a b-e-a-u in my hair, and I said a b-e-a-u, she replied, "That would be awfully large to put in your hair!" The whole class's laughter stung more than a swarm of bees, and though it was probably forgotten by everyone else in a moment, it throbbed in my mind.

Like the other students who had been recalcitrant about learning their spelling words, I had to stay in from recess to learn them. I was not accustomed to being in the group of those who did not do what they were supposed to do. I vowed never again to let myself get in that predicament because of incomplete assignments. What was a throwaway comment by my teacher, which she never intended as hurtful, annihilated my ability to trust her, especially because she had been the one to initiate the bargain about limiting study time. I had tried to do what my teacher proposed, and it resulted in my getting even less of the acceptance and approval I sought.

I wanted to be a doer, like my father, so the focus of my learning became the acquisition of skills. He liked to help my brother and me learn many new skills, gain confidence in our ability, and participate with others in some of the activities that had not been available to him when he was a child.

One winter we each got our first pair of ice skates. We bundled up and went down to the lake. My father put on his ice skates first and figured out how to use them. Brooklyn born and raised, he had never ice skated before in his life, but after about 15 minutes he felt confident enough to bring us out on the ice to teach us.

Having been a professional saxophonist since he was a teenager, music was an important part of who my father was. He organized bands with my brother, my cousins, and me, and we would rehearse each weekend. Our signature song was *Voláre*, and we performed at the school talent show. My father's delight in our performance and his enthusiasm as he rehearsed us underscored my connection with him through music. I enjoyed our closeness at these times and I realized that my achievement in playing the piano resulted in a very satisfying link with my father.

My father's reaction to my fears about any form of inadequate performance was to help me do better. When I was afraid that I would strike out in softball games at school, my father responded by spending hours pitching to me so that I could become a competent batter. I came to believe that my intelligence and willingness to work hard would be the keys to my success. Although learning skills in many arenas is very important, I needed to develop a sense of self-worth and purpose that would always be with me, even when I couldn't be especially skillful or solve problems by working hard.

Learning that we may be accepted because we are, not because of what we do, was a lesson a long time in coming for me. I think it was when I started teaching first grade and had those feelings of acceptance for each of my students that I began to rethink my childhood belief that acceptance had to be earned by high achievement. I realized that I cared about my students, not because of what they achieved, but just because. Because I felt that way about them, it dawned on me that others, especially my parents, had felt that way about me. I wish I had been able to see that at the time. Making sure my students saw it became a major focus of my teaching and leading.

Realizing Our Resources

Realizations about acceptance influenced me to help others—both children and adults—know and accept themselves, rather than try to please others in order to be accepted. I encourage teachers to note their own natural inclinations. What are they drawn to or whom? What evokes their passion? How do they express themselves when they are not self-censoring? What are their core values? As a leader, I notice the talents and interests of individuals and acknowledge them. I try to facilitate further exploration or use of these gifts. It is very exciting to watch staff members use their individual talents and interests to the benefit of the school community. As a principal, I can sometimes offer resources, as well as the opportunity for the staff to implement their ideas.

When I first became a principal, my youth and some of the staff's intentionally hurtful behaviors toward me made it difficult for me to foster a culture of support. As time passed and my staying power became evident, teachers were more willing to work with me to address schoolwide issues. Once we pooled our resources, we achieved so much that they reluctantly began to concede that perhaps I could facilitate their growth through recognition of their skills and support of their initiatives.

In my next principalships, many staff members were much more receptive to my efforts to foster a culture of support, and we began to collaborate much sooner. My role as a leader was often less visible, because I worked behind the scenes to promote the talents and endeavors of staff members. Sometimes my endorsement of their ideas was all that was required and they virtually did the rest by themselves.

For example, an art teacher had the idea to feature students' creations throughout the town during the school year, as well as at special events. She and the other art teachers also came up with the idea of an art retrospective. Students wrote reflections on their art over their 5 years in school to accompany an exhibit of examples of their growth. Our art teacher even triple-matted students' creations before displaying them, conveying her respect for their artwork. Families, teachers, and fellow students were enthralled.

Another teacher was remarkably adept at involving students in drama and musical productions that gave the youngsters opportunities to shine in ways that had not been revealed previously. Because the productions were very high caliber, students were deservedly proud of their stage roles, as well as their involvement in such a valued school production.

In one school, two teachers were remarkably gifted in their ability to promote common goals by bringing the community together. For example, they conceptualized and organized our "Turkey Trot," gathering the whole school population in the auditorium to lead us in song and warm-ups before we went outdoors to walk, jog, or run. They recruited parents to keep us safe by directing traffic in the neighborhood and to supply orange slices and water. One of the teachers even physically symbolized the community spirit they had fostered by appearing as a huge, brightly colored turkey. By appearing in costume, he stepped out of his own identity to serve as a unifying image.

Many other teachers make contributions to school communities in ways that are more subtle and less visible to everyone else. Their enthusiasm and responsiveness, their participation in the initiatives of their colleagues, and the way they inspire students in their classrooms are known and valued by the school community.

Many teachers have been mentors to our new faculty, spending countless hours familiarizing new colleagues with our school culture and the expectations of the community. One teacher organized a welcoming breakfast and provided the food, decorations, and party favors herself.

Leadership that supports and nurtures is a large part of what builds such a strong sense of community. Identifying and acknowledging the specific talents of adults in the school helps them to share their gifts; this promotes their growth, as well as that of others.

You can tell when staff feel supported by their principal and peers by their motivation and the warm feeling that they exude in the school. Being recognized for what is special about them brings a deeper sense of acceptance and results in each person then bringing more of themselves into their roles in the school. When the staff feel seen, known, and understood, the whole school flourishes.

On Common Ground

This sense of community and focus on individuality takes time to build. When I first became a principal, I was not aware of how gradual a process it would need to be.

That first year, when it came time to do evaluations of teachers, I created evaluation packets and distributed them to all the teachers. I asked the teachers to write their "philosophy of education" and "growth plans" for the coming year. My intent was to acknowledge that it wouldn't be fair for me to walk into classrooms and make judgments about performance without first ascertaining what the teachers were trying to do. I wanted to show my support of their own goal setting, and believed that this would be an appropriately respectful process for evaluating teachers.

I wanted to offer something to an experienced staff, many of whom had been teachers far longer than I. I had thought of my evaluation packet as an opportunity for self-reflection and dialogue, and hoped that could be one of my contributions. However, the teachers nearly had a fit when they read what I had written, and although I heard their responses, I couldn't believe my ears.

"Growth plan! Philosophy of education! What does she think we're doing here?"

"I don't have time to sit around and write all this stuff."

"She's the principal. Let her come in and evaluate me. That's her job. It's not my job to write a thesis for her!"

My efforts to explain my thinking or clarify my intentions were not helpful. Yet I firmly believed that to walk in "cold" and make judgments would be a setup for all of us. If I was judging performance based on criteria we hadn't discussed, how could they be expected to meet my expectations? How would I know what they, in turn, hoped I would see and comment on?

I insisted that people try my process and that we would see how it worked. I hoped that the teachers would see that it wasn't a trick, but rather an earnest attempt to promote dialogue about what they were doing and why. However, my attempts to engage people mostly resulted in stony silence or begrudging answers that revealed as little as possible about the individual. No one seemed interested in discussing teaching methodology or philosophy. After a while I felt defeated and just wanted to get the evaluations done. "Maybe another year will be better, after people see that I'm not out to get them," I told myself.

In retrospect, I think that the teachers may have feared being evaluated on what they wrote as their philosophy and growth plan. I think they felt that the evaluation itself would begin the minute they put pen to paper, even though my intention had been to use the growth plan as a way for them to express their individuality, their challenges, and their goals. The evaluation of their performance would come afterward.

Ironically, it was something totally unrelated that helped us build relationships. I got married. You may wonder what this has to do with anything. So did I.

When the teachers found out that I was planning to get married, they had a shower for me, and their warmth surprised me even more than did the event itself. I started to realize that by getting married I was choosing to do something that most of them also had done. We would now have something in common. It was that simple.

Years later, at a faculty meeting, I shared with the teachers a poem I had written, and it created quite a stir:

I have a new growth plan of which you should know.
It's something quite special, and beginning to show.
As with a good growth plan, a goal is the start,
And ways to achieve it, these come from the heart.
This plan involved people; it's not achieved alone.

The involvement of others has already shown.
It will mean temporary changes in our school and how it's run.
I need your help and ideas so that it's satisfactorily done.
Our work is education, and for that we need the student.
With enrollments so declining, I'm doing what is prudent—
I'm growing one!

When the teachers realized I was pregnant, they talked with me about their experiences when they had been pregnant. They offered suggestions and advice. There was another shower, this time for the baby. I still cherish the cradle that was commissioned by the teachers and made by one teacher's husband.

What I had not been able to do through the language of growth plans and goal statements was happening in other ways. We were growing closer as we realized that there were things that were similar about us, in addition to the obvious differences. I could feel their skepticism melting away. We were learning to trust each other.

I'm not recommending getting pregnant as the solution to poor relationships with the staff. That would be a bit extreme. Yet I learned a powerful lesson about the many unexpected ways there may be to achieve the goal of building relationships with staff.

I had not considered the importance of how different I seemed to the staff when I first became principal. The teachers had gotten stuck in thinking about the ways that we were different, and they focused on trying to keep their school as it was before I arrived. I was focused on our working together for the good of the students, and had given much less consideration to finding ways to build bridges so the staff and I could come together. I now better understand how activities like talking about sports or sharing recipes may serve larger organizational goals. They are ways that people make connections. Once those connections are forged, colleagues then may collaborate on educational issues.

The benefit of having been a principal for so many years is that I can now see what was not evident to me at the beginning of my career—what would have helped us connect more quickly. As important as it was for me to establish myself in ways that were congruent with my beliefs, it was crucial that I discover what we had in common and build relationships from this common ground.

To Stand Up, to Stand Behind

Finding commonalities can help new principals connect with their staff, and these connections are often solidified when there is a threat from outside the group. However, when the principal is new, the principal may be viewed as the outsider. I remember such a situation from my second year as a teacher. The principal had been newly appointed and was about to discover how the existing faculty would become unified through their opposition to their new leader.

There was a specialist in this school whom teachers reported had very little control of the classes she taught. Although she was dedicated to her specialty, the students did not follow her instructions, sometimes running around the classrooms and even standing on desks. Teachers complained to the principal. Finally, in the spring, word got out that the principal had recommended that the teacher not be rehired. Suddenly everyone was outraged by his action, and a petition was circulated among the teachers, stating to the principal that the teacher was outstanding and definitely an asset to the school.

I had just become a teacher the year before and wanted very much to feel a solidarity with my colleagues. I was trying to learn from them what it meant to be a professional educator. Yet I had heard them bad-mouth the teacher, and now they were saying things that directly contradicted their own previous statements.

I felt that I should speak up, but I was afraid to alienate my new colleagues. I really didn't have to take a stand, because untenured teachers had not been asked to sign the petition, possibly jeopardizing their own job security. However, I felt that what was happening was wrong. The compromise that I worked out with myself was to speak privately with the principal. I told him about the petition he was about to receive and my discomfort with it. I explained my bewilderment about the whole situation and said that I felt guilty for not confronting my new colleagues. He appreciated my sentiments and told me that he didn't expect me to voice my concern to them.

Being in his first year as principal, he, too, was bewildered. He questioned the teachers' commitment when they changed their stories about this teacher's competence after he had taken the very action they had been suggesting all year. His recommendation ultimately was accepted by the superintendent and the school committee, yet I believe our principal was disheartened by the staff's response.

In my own principalships, I have had similar experiences with teachers complaining about a colleague's behavior, demanding I do something about it, and then disowning their role and opinions when asked if they knew what had prompted my actions. I learned to act only on what I saw or what was reported by people who would be willing to discuss it publicly. I also realized how beneficial it was for me when people remembered what they had seen me do in the past and reconsidered the likelihood of whatever unfair actions were being attributed to me.

One teacher who sensed the frustration and pain I was experiencing about a difficult situation at school wrote me the following letter. I saved it because it reflected the teacher's understanding of some of the dynamics of leadership.

> I came here because you are the leader for whom I want to work. You have always made it a point to show your support and recognition. I, too, hope you feel my support . . . . But superior leaders don't always win the endorsement of the majority. When perspectives aren't agreed upon, there is always a chance that people will misunderstand one another. What is important is that you stand behind your beliefs. I believe that you do that with diplomacy and grace.

Lee's words were a great comfort. I didn't expect Lee to do or say anything publicly. The letter indicated an awareness and validation that provided me with the private support I needed.

Essence

Every year I send out a letter to all the adults in our school community. I write the letter at the end of the summer, sharing my reflections on the connection between learning and something I did during the summer. I mail the letter to the staff about a week before school begins and put it in the "first day of school" packet for families. It is my way of welcoming people back to school and sharing a little about myself.

I never know how most people react to my letters because they don't tell me. I imagine that some people glance at my letter and if they haven't found them interesting in the past, throw it away. Others may read it out of personal curiosity but be less interested in the connections I make between my experiences and education. Some may be annoyed that I send it at all. I am aware of these possibilities, yet I do write it each year because I hope that there are some for whom it is a welcome invitation to a new school year.

My letters are personal and informal. They are not the "It's September, let's get out the apples" type of communication. They are different. I know that. I want them to be different. In fact, sending these letters at all is a bit unusual, but it feels important to me, and I work to write something worth reading. One year, this is what I wrote:

After putting on my swimsuit and critically eyeing my reflection in our bedroom mirror at Squam Lake, I went to the dock for a swim. It was usually my practice to swim back and forth to the point, so that someone on the dock or someone who was swimming would be nearby if I got in trouble. Henry wanted to go up to the house in a little while, but he assured me that my voice would carry if I called for help.

I headed out and found myself swimming very close to two loons in our cove. Loons don't usually stay that close to people, so I was amazed that they continued their search for food so near to me. After each of them put their head underwater in search of food, they would make a sound very different than their usual haunting wail. The previous night, Henry and I listened to that sound and wondered what they were communicating. Today Henry called out to me that the sound must be a compliment, and I was touched by his sweetness. The loons and I swam together a little longer, and then they went their way and I went mine.

Thomson's beach was my goal, but when I got there I felt so good that I kept on going. I was enjoying my solitary swim, feeling the warmth of the sun on my face. My stroke was propelling me through the water and I glided past the trees along the shore. Becoming so attuned with the natural environment, I was momentarily stunned by a Squam Lake tour boat approaching me. Though I felt annoyed by the intrusion, I waved at the people in the boat and smiled more broadly when the tour guide told me that they had thought I was a mermaid.

Perhaps this 46-year-old body wasn't as worthy of my self-criticism as I had thought. At least my husband and the gray-haired tour guide didn't think so, having just found two unique ways to convey their approval. As I swam, the word "acceptance" came to mind, and I mentally repeated it in time with my strokes. Acceptance, acceptance, I thought as I glided through the water and felt more and more content. I felt peaceful and strong, continuing to swim much further than I had ever gone before.

"Maybe I'll swim to that rock," I thought, as I moved through the lake, keeping pace with the movement of the clouds overhead. "I'm already there; I think I'll keep on going." The more I thought about acceptance, the further I swam. I made it all the way to Little Heron Cove! I couldn't believe it.

Reflecting on my experience, I realized that I was energized by the feeling of acceptance and actually able to do more because of the freedom. I want to remember this awareness because I believe it will help me, and perhaps others, to come closer to reaching our potential in ways that feel congruent with our essence.

Sincerely,
Susan Villani

I knew my letter that year was a little "out there," because I mentioned my critical reaction to seeing my image as I wore my bathing suit. That is a little unusual for a principal to be discussing. Yet with all the concern we have as a society about being thin and beautiful, it didn't seem too outrageous to acknowledge that I am also susceptible to those pressures. Although my feelings of self-acceptance initially were triggered by comments from my husband and the tour guide, hopefully what I learned from my experience will enable me to prompt myself to be more self-accepting in the future.

There was a bit more feedback than usual to my letter that year. Some staff members remarked that they enjoyed it and thought about what I wrote. A few parents were very enthusiastic about it after they received it on the first day of school. One mother told me that she was so impressed by my letter that she read it to her son, discussing it with him afterward.

"I loved your letter!" one father called out to me as I was driving through the center of town. I noticed that I was surprised to hear that comment from a man, catching myself in the assumption that it would be women who would relate more strongly to a message about self-acceptance, particularly because it involved "body acceptance."

Then I got a call from the superintendent of schools asking me if I had heard about Sally's letter to him and the school committee. I braced myself for I knew not what and replied, "No, I haven't. What does it say?"

"She's ripping about your letter," was the gist of his response.

I was flabbergasted. "What does she say is wrong with it?" The superintendent couldn't tell me, because Sally had not been specific.

I asked the superintendent if he would like a copy of the letter to see if he thought it was objectionable. He said that she had attached a copy of my letter to her own, so he had already seen it. "Susan, you have to admit it is a little unusual."

"Sure it is," I answered, "but so what? I have done other things that are unusual and they have benefited the school. I send a personal letter to everyone at the end of every summer. Do you see anything in particular that would be so offensive to a parent in this one?" He didn't, and said that he had discussed it with a school committee member, who noted its uniqueness, but also didn't understand what was such a problem.

The superintendent suggested that I call Sally and ask her, which is exactly what I had intended to do. Sally and I had worked together on many school-related projects. I knew her to be an intelligent and articulate person who stands behind what she believes. When I reached her, I said that I heard she was offended by my letter and I was calling to find out what it was that she found objectionable.

You could have knocked me over with a feather when I heard Sally's response. It was something like, "Oh Susan. Come on. Essence? Your essence? If someone gets ahold of this letter and reads it at town meeting, there won't be any way that we can defend the school budget to the community with a principal writing a letter like this."

I thought for a moment. Even if I had done something outrageous, which I hadn't, I couldn't believe that the townspeople would refuse to pass the school budget. They might look to the superintendent to address my performance, but they wouldn't take out their frustrations on all of the children in town. It was clear to me that Sally was attributing far more weight to my letter than was warranted.

I told her that I was sorry that she felt that way and that I would think about it, because if she felt that way, there were probably others who had that same reaction. I went back and reread the letter, trying to see things from her perspective. "Essence." "Congruent with our essence." I didn't get it. That seemed fairly innocuous to me. It was another way of saying "true to ourselves." As I thought about it more, I wondered whether it was really the word "essence" that bothered her, or rather its context: the principal looking at her body in the mirror and then swimming and thinking about self-acceptance.

I heard more about the letter each day. I showed it to a few people I respected and asked for their responses. They too were puzzled by the intensity of the feedback I got from Sally. I was disappointed that she hadn't told me her concerns before speaking to the superintendent and the school committee. I realized that she probably did represent a segment of readers who didn't like the letter. Receiving positive feedback about my letter from parents, almost on a daily basis, helped validate my belief in the value of what I had done.

Yet there was a difference in my response to this event than to others in the past. This time, I didn't see anything wrong with what I did, and if I had it to do over again, I would. I wouldn't refrain from writing and sending the letter, and I didn't feel scared or sorry. I actually felt empowered by my self-assurance on this issue.

If talking about self-acceptance is so disturbing, then I think we have a lot of work ahead of us. Girls as young as 8 years old are succumbing to anorexia and bulimia, teens are committing suicide at alarming rates, and many people abuse alcohol and drugs, in part because they are not comfortable with themselves. We had better start talking more about self-acceptance. In fact, the amount and intensity of people's reactions to my letter confirmed that I had touched on something people needed to think about.

Modeling What's Important

In the summer letter, I had chosen to tell a story about myself, sharing my thoughts and feelings about an issue I considered relevant to a school community. Even if the feedback had been largely negative, I would not have regretted writing my letter. In healthy organizations and communities, disagreement is part of constructive communication and growth. I welcome people's reactions and feelings about all aspects of my leadership and about our school, but where I draw the line is if I am told I should not be myself in the process of being the principal.

If there comes a time when a principal's philosophy is not shared by the majority of the school community, then the principal has a decision to make: either move closer to what the community feels it needs or find a school community in which the match is more congruent. As principal, it is not my job to take the safe path, making sure never to do anything that is controversial.

A principal must be ready, I believe, to influence a school community about educational issues. If there are too many people who don't want for their children what the principal strives to provide, then the principal may no longer be as effective.

I must admit that there are times when I wonder if the extra tasks I initiate are worth the time and effort. Sending out the summer letters is an additional job to be done at a busy time. Yet each time I consider abandoning such a practice, I remember that I have established a tradition of summer letters. Many in our school community have told me that they look forward to receiving them.

My role is to promote thinking, among adults as well as children. I feel proud when the staff and I have created an environment that is a welcoming, friendly place, where children can feel safe to learn. We have worked to make sure that differences are acceptable, and in so doing it becomes safe for each of us—students, teachers, staff, and administrator—to be ourselves.

As educators and parents, we know the importance of modeling for children. To be comfortable as role models, we must be accepting of ourselves and confident about what we have to offer. Parents and teachers are daily models for children. As an elementary school principal, I am also in a position to be a model as a leader, a woman, a learner, a risk taker, and someone who is comfortable having feelings and sharing them.

When children share their perceptions of me, I can see easily which messages have come through. Adrian, a third-grader, once came to my office to tell me about a poetry anthology done at his previous school. I agreed that it was a good idea, and suggested he speak with our language arts specialist. He continued telling me about the anthology and why it would be good for our school. After several attempts to get him to speak with the person who might act

Figure 5.1. "Women Can Be Good Principals" poster. Created by and reproduced with permission of Jennifer L. Nardone.

on his suggestion, I said, "You don't seem to want to speak with her. Why not?"

Adrian smiled patiently at me and explained, "When I told you that I speak another language and that my picture should be included on the ESL display, it happened. I figure you are the person to talk to if I want to see something get done." Clearly, for this student I was a principal who acts on ideas.

Another student expressed her belief that "women can be good principals" in the caption of a poster she created for our Career Exploration Program. My office was pictured, including the chairs arranged on the braided rug, ready for student dialogue. For this student, the principal is approachable and helps students solve problems together.

When your actions reflect your philosophy, you are modeling what you hope children will learn. There are additional steps you can take to concretize their perceptions. The following examples are from my experience.

After I earned my doctorate in educational administration, I decided to use the title "doctor" in school. I wanted the students to become as accustomed to calling a woman "doctor" as they would be to calling a man "doctor." I just had to make sure that they didn't think I was going to give them painful injections or bad-tasting medicine. I wanted them to understand how much studying is required to be a principal, and what an important job it is to be the leader of a school.

Each year I include something in my weekly schedule that involves learning something new. One year it was taking flute lessons with some fifth-graders and being a member of our school band. Another year I was an art student with the same class for an entire school year, facing the same challenges and feeling the same satisfaction when my work resulted in a product I was proud to see displayed. I think it's important for students to see adults in situations that greatly challenge them and for the adults to be able to share their frustration as well as their elation.

Every year in one school, we took our fifth-grade students away for 3 days for an outdoor education experience. When I climbed up a tree and walked across a cable on the high ropes course, students saw me as a learner and risk taker—in the same position they were in. One year I was so frightened by being 50 feet up in the air that when I came down, I started crying.

"Why are you crying, Dr. Villani? You did it and you're down now."

I replied, "Because it was very scary and my mind hasn't caught up with my body. But it sure was a great feeling to do it." I was experiencing several emotions simultaneously: fear, pride, and exhilaration. I wanted students to see that we all have those feelings and that it is all right to show them.

I also want to be a role model for students about writing. I think that the written word is very powerful. The summer letter I wrote elicited strong reactions from people. Many told me that they related to the feelings I was describing or that they thought a lot about what I wrote. So the letter was a good example of the impact words may have on people. When Sally wrote about my summer letter, she was capitalizing on the power of writing. She may have modeled for her own children the importance of being able to express herself so clearly and emphatically. It is imperative that our students learn how to think and be able to express their ideas through their writing, as well as through their speaking and actions.

Each year, right before the end of school, I give students a pen with an inscription about satisfaction in knowing they gave their very best at school and at home. I go to every class to hand out my small gifts to the children. "I think writing is very important," I told them one year. "I hope that these pens will remind you to keep writing during the summer. Write a letter or a postcard, write in your journal, write a poem, write a shopping list if you must, but keep writing." The children laughed when I got to the part about the shopping list, and I knew that they understood my point.

If the students heard that a letter I wrote elicited powerful reactions (and we know that children do hear things that their parents whisper to keep from their ears), they saw a real-life illustration that the written word is a very powerful tool. Even if the children knew nothing about the substance of the letter, they will have known that I followed my own advice to them and wrote during the summer. Maybe in the future when they have a strong feeling, they will write a letter, a poem, a book, or an editorial and share it.

Recognizing and Owning Our Part

Most writing involves reflection, but there are also times when people need to speak up in the moment, without the luxury of time to prepare carefully what they will say.

I remember a time when there was a big commotion after recess because a student had pulled down another student's shorts while they were playing outside. After hearing from the recess supervisors and the classroom teachers, I interviewed each of the identified students individually. Daniel readily admitted his guilt and the seriousness of his offense. He already understood why what he had done was wrong. Yet as he took responsibility for his misbehavior, he confided, "I know I shouldn't have done it. But they were saying, 'Do it! Do it!' and after a while I just gave in."

The other students who were involved all pointed fingers at each other, but only Patrick admitted he was part of the group that goaded Daniel to "pants" the other child. After consulting with several colleagues in our school, I took a very strong position. I punished all the children involved to the same degree.

I told them that Daniel did something very wrong, yet he admitted his wrongdoing and took responsibility for his actions. The others influenced him, but they did not own their part of the result. I told them that a value of our school community is that people not be bystanders to hurtful or prejudicial behaviors without speaking up or taking some other action. Bystanders who don't object are as responsible for the hurts to victims as are the original perpetrators. This is a concept that sometimes even children's parents are not prepared to accept.

I called the boys' parents to let them know about the incident. I told each of them that I knew their sons and that I didn't believe any of them would have behaved individually as they had when they were together that day at recess. Then I told them of my decision to give each of the children a half-day, in-house suspension and loss of recess for a week.

Some parents supported my decision. Others, at least, accepted it, but some of the parents were outraged. How could I punish their child, who had not committed the act, to the same degree that I punished the one who had? They spoke heatedly with me and later with each other about the unfairness of my decision. In fact, it became quite the topic of conversation for a couple of days, and their anger was reenergized as they spoke with one another.

In a meeting with the staff, I told them what had happened and what I had decided. They were being approached by parents, and I wanted them to know the full story before they responded. The teachers and noon aides supported my position, both with students and with parents. In fact, some publicly vocalized their support of my decision. We were all troubled that some parents were unwilling to let their children take, or learn to take, responsibility for their actions. I also think that because the teachers had seen me support them when they had made difficult decisions and were criticized, they now were doing the same thing for me.

One parent approached me in the hallway a couple of days later. She said that she had heard about the incident the night before from several disgruntled parents. "I told them that I agreed with your position. Someday our daughters will be with these boys in a bar or on dates. We will be very glad to know that these boys learned about not getting swept up in a group mentality that gets them to do things they've been taught not to do. We will want them to have learned from this lesson when they are out with our daughters." This parent understood precisely why I felt so strongly that I needed to respond quickly and firmly to the boys about the seriousness of betraying their own values because of a group dynamic.

Later that day, I was given reason to pause when I heard from Patrick's mother. She explained that she and her husband had been totally prepared to support what I had done, but when they spoke with Patrick, they learned that he had removed himself from the other boys when he couldn't get them to stop what they were doing. She didn't think Patrick should be treated the same way as the other boys, because he had chosen a different action. By walking away, Patrick had made his own statement about the wrongness of their actions. After all, it would have been asking a great deal to expect a 9-year-old to go get an adult when his friends were behaving poorly, even though we would encourage him to do that in the future.

Now I had a lot to think about. Because there were other parents who felt strongly that the boys' punishment was too harsh, if I changed my decision for Patrick, they would surely expect me to reverse it for their sons too. Yet what Patrick's mother said to me made sense. I consulted with a couple of colleagues and they agreed with me that I should modify Patrick's punishment in recognition of his behavior. I knew that I had to consider what was in his best interest, even if it meant that there would be a backlash from others afterward. I met with Patrick, told him I had reconsidered, and rescinded his in-house suspension. He readily agreed to miss the recesses. I apologized for my initial judgment and told Patrick I was wrong. I told him I was influenced greatly by his mother's call, because she helped me to see that he had taken a stand and had not been a willing bystander to the situation.

During the boys' in-house suspensions, I spoke with each of them privately. I said that I knew what kind of people they were and was sure that this would not have happened had they been alone. I emphasized my concern that the group had greater power at the moment of the incident than each of them had exercised individually and that I wanted them to learn now, in a safe place, how to handle themselves in the future. I concluded with each boy by saying that I felt certain that he would learn from this and not be as likely to act based on pressure from a group in the future. Each one signaled to me, in his own way, that he understood what I was talking about. The boys were actually more accepting of my reaction than some of their parents had been.

The students knew that I valued them very much. It was their behavior at the moment that I disliked. My confidence in their future behavior reassured them and I made sure to signal each of them several times over the next week that what had happened was over and I still cared about them. There would be no grudges on my part nor, I believe, on theirs.

I worked hard to reestablish good relationships with some of their parents, who remained critical of my decision. In fact, I never did hear from the other parents about my reversal of Patrick's punishment. Perhaps the other boys knew that it was fair and didn't tell their parents. They weren't hoping for a change in their consequences. Children usually do have a strong sense of fairness, even if they get carried away in the moment. I respected the boys for how they handled their own punishments.

If we ask children to take a stand, and expect other adults to do it, we must be prepared to do it as well. Part of being authentic is being willing to act on what we believe in, even if we are initially uncomfortable doing so. As leaders, we must model this behavior for those we lead.

It matters to me that we create a school community where people are accepted and protected. Although we may criticize or even punish someone for specific behaviors, we must not condemn the person. Not only do we not want to treat individuals that way, but we also need to remember to focus on what's best for the whole school community. People must know that they belong "just because." They need to be certain that disagreements or misbehaviors may bring some specific consequence but will not jeopardize their sense of belonging in the school community.

CHAPTER **6**

Mentors, Allies, and Friends: Support for Authentic Leadership and Vision

A dear friend gave me a calendar as a gift to mark the new year. I scratched my head in puzzlement when I saw the cover picture of a scantily clad woman who was mountain climbing. What on earth was my friend thinking when she selected this for me? She was surprised that it hadn't been obvious to me. "You have been a mentor, a coach to me in so many ways. I remember you struggling with things that seemed insurmountable, and then using those accomplishments to fortify you for your next endeavors. I can actually hear you urging me to do what I need to do, with full confidence that I will be successful. Of course I chose the 'Women Who Climb' calendar for you. I don't care what that woman was wearing; she represented how you challenge yourself and others to go the next step."

In Support of Leaders

Part of leading well is identifying, finding, and accepting the support we need. Support for a leader may come from a colleague, a parent, someone from the community, or a friend. Sometimes it even comes

83

from a child. Support may be for the leader's feelings or may be about a current situation. Support may take the form of hand holding, help in strategizing, modeling, or mentoring. Wherever we find it and whatever form it takes, it is crucial that we surround ourselves with enough of the kind of support we need to do our jobs well and to be who we are, which means knowing—or learning—what that is.

When I doubt myself, I like to look in a file I keep in my desk that contains letters of support. Reading the letters helps me remember that there are folks who appreciate me and value what I do. After a particularly trying episode at school, receiving the following letter from a parent (with a bag of jellybeans), made all the difference:

> It's your vision that attracts the excellent teachers and staff. . . . Your standards are high, you demand a great deal, and you want the best for your students, families, and teachers. . . . Like me, you are willing to take risks and therefore draw controversy. However, you handle controversy much better than I do. In fact . . . when I want to back away or ignore conflict, you encourage—and sometimes make—me deal with it. I treasure your ability to inspire me to rise to the occasion. . . . Because you can inspire and teach someone as stubborn as I am, I'm confident about your ability to lead the rest of the school.

One of the most crucial comments of support I've received was from the person who supervised me in my first principalship. During the many difficulties I faced when I began, the faith of the superintendent was a big part of what sustained me. When I went into his office to tell him that the faculty had filed a second grievance against me, my composure shattered, and I began to cry. "I don't know how this can be happening," I told him, "I'm trying so hard."

He reassured me by saying, "Sometimes getting a grievance is not because you are doing things wrong, but because you are doing things right!" Still, I cannot imagine a more encouraging response. Knowing the superintendent could see beyond the turmoil of the moment and support my courage enabled me to use my energy to be a better leader.

Talking with close friends was another important support. How many hours I spent in a dear friend's kitchen, regaling her with my latest travails. I cried, and sometimes we laughed, as I told her what it was like trying to be a principal. Her consistent faith in me, as well as her outrage at what she was hearing about my new colleagues, helped sustain me through that gut-wrenching time.

At the Core of Leadership

At a workshop for administrators, I first heard about the NorthEast Coalition of Education Leaders (NECEL), which has contributed enormously to my evolution as a leader. During my first few agonizing years as a principal, I met women administrators who helped me understand—and withstand—my daily experiences. Many of us were grappling with how to get more women into administrative jobs and then how to succeed in them. NECEL members offered just what I needed at the time: support, advice, and different models of leadership.

One NECEL member was even a model for me about being a principal and starting a family. I literally ran to talk with her at a NECEL conference when I heard she had had a child and continued in her position.

Not only did NECEL contribute to my evolution as a leader, NECEL also had its own evolution, as NECEL members tried to communicate how we do the job differently. From this came NECEL's articulation of the five attributes of leadership: caring, collaboration, courage, intuition, and vision. Though I couldn't have articulated these attributes at the time, they reflected the traits in myself I called upon to be a leader. Had I known that others, too, recognized these attributes as being at the core of leadership, I would have been more confident about openly using them in my new role as principal. A relationship I had with a teacher during my first 2 years as a principal illustrates the power of these attributes.

Dolores disagreed with just about everything I did as the principal of the school. Her judgments often seemed harsh and undeserved. She was a very witty, charismatic person, and the combination of these qualities and her judgments often left me feeling defenseless and publicly shamed. For many months, I had a recurring dream that Dolores changed her opinion of me. Each time I awoke, I was confronted with the futility of my wish. I still find it hard to admit how much I hoped it would happen.

When Dolores casually mentioned her wish to leave teaching and begin a career in business, I offered to advise her on ways to move into the private sector. We talked about how she might present her credentials, and I told her the benefits of "information interviewing." I also told her I had no doubt she would be successful in her new career.

Weeks later, Dolores told me how much the information interviewing was helping her break into the field. That afternoon I got a note, spontaneously written on yellow classroom paper:

"You know so much. What a waste of two years."

I couldn't believe my eyes. I probably blinked to make sure I wasn't asleep. Dolores had acknowledged my strengths! Had I withheld my knowledge and advice, she never would have expressed what I had wanted so badly to hear her say. Though I couldn't have articulated the NECEL attributes at the time, they reflected how I worked.

My vision of a school community was that all members would find their work satisfying and fulfilling and would receive colleagues' support toward this end, regardless of their personal feelings about the individuals. Intuitively I sensed that this could be a way to begin the kind of respectful relationship Dolores and I had not been able to have before. My caring took the form of offering advice and knowledge beyond my responsibility as a principal. It took courage to offer assistance to Dolores. It took even more courage not merely to advise her, but also to offer to collaborate with her in her next steps.

These attributes of leadership are often present in leaders who are nontraditional. Whether it is men or women who are new administrators, people of color, or administrators who seek alternative ways to lead, articulating what they do is both affirming and instructive.

Doing Something More

Although people had recognized these attributes of leadership in me in other ways throughout my life, my path to leadership in public elementary schools has been a little unusual. School administration had never been my dream.

In my late teens, I had strongly resisted my mother's urging to become a teacher. I kept saying that I didn't want to work only with women and children, resisting a career that was typically prescribed for my gender. I felt like I should "do something more."

I had been led to believe, by my parents and teachers, that I was intelligent and talented and that I was capable of excelling in a prestigious field. Because society didn't hold the teaching profession in high esteem, I closed myself off from the idea of teaching, intuiting that no matter how well I performed, I would not be sufficiently recognized for my achievement.

At my father's suggestion, I majored in business administration in college and discovered that I was one of only two female students in the department. When I was about to graduate, I heard that women were not being offered management training positions but instead had to take secretarial jobs and work their way up. I was so outraged by that idea that I decided to get a master's degree in higher education administration, mistakenly believing that gender discrimination would not be a factor at the college level.

Yet when I applied to graduate school, I did so in elementary education. How did that happen when I was so adamant about not wanting to be a teacher? Perhaps in a time of uncertainty, I went back to what seemed safe and familiar: my mother's suggestion to become a teacher.

In my second year of teaching first grade, I offered to teach our newly appointed principal about the educational needs of young children and to give him feedback on his entry into our school community. He welcomed my offer and I unknowingly took another step toward becoming a principal myself. His acknowledgment that I knew more than he about early childhood education, as well as the interpersonal dynamics of our school, affirmed my self-confidence and empowered me to begin to think of myself as an educational leader.

During the next few years, that principal and the superintendent told me that I would be an excellent principal. I scoffed at the idea. When they insisted, I told them that I loved teaching first grade and that I thought administration was a horrible job. It was too bad that they had to do it, I said, but I was perfectly content where I was. They persisted, and at one point the superintendent said something that resonated within me: "If you value community as much as you seem to, you could influence a larger community as a principal than you could as a teacher of one class."

The idea that I could influence an entire school community was very enticing. At one point the superintendent predicted that I would move on within a year or two and said that was the reason that he canceled my presentation to the school committee of my proposal for a teacher center.

In fact, one year later I was appointed to a principalship in a neighboring state. I was amazed that the superintendent had known me better than I knew myself. How could he have foreseen my future when I was so unaware of my growing interest in school administration? The effect that principal and superintendent had on my career development and aspirations was significant. They clearly saw something in me that I hadn't seen in myself.

Not a Fairy Godmother

Sometimes there is someone who has a vision of us that surpasses our current aspirations. Gail Sheehy calls this heightened vision "the Dream." People may support us in this journey to realize our Dream without our initial awareness that they are doing it.

During my first principalship, I was invited to join the Education Subcommittee of the Governor's Advisory Commission on Women. I didn't know what prompted the invitation, but I was intrigued and delighted. I needed a change of pace and an opportunity to think about education in a more global way. The women I met at the first meeting were dynamic and articulate. They were doing all kinds of interesting things throughout the state, in many different roles and institutions.

Before I knew it, I was offered support for an endeavor I had only briefly mentioned. A liaison from the state department of education offered to provide technical assistance and funding for our Career Exploration Program. I jumped at the offer.

It was only afterward, when I was asked to write a booklet describing this endeavor as a model for the state, that I found out that I had been recommended specifically for support. I felt like I had a fairy godmother. In fact, it was a very real person—the Chair of the Education Subcommittee of the Governor's Advisory Commission on Women—who chose to sponsor me. When I think about the camaraderie and support I received from the members of the Education Subcommittee, I still feel a deep sense of protection because, despite what was happening at my school, I had these strong and accomplished women on my side.

The image of a fairy godmother or a prince charming, who comes to rescue the helpless novice, represents, I believe, a longing that many of us occasionally feel. Even though passive longing may be effective in fairy tales, in the real world, novices need to learn to act on their own behalf. Fairy godmothers rescue; mentors empower.

A mentor is someone who combines the skills and caring of professional colleagues, supporters, and allies with a knowledge about ways our talents may be utilized professionally. A mentor consistently believes in our capability and commits to working with us to further our professional growth.

A mentor looks realistically at the situation and speaks honestly, without glossing over the difficult issues. A mentor works with us in the hard times, the unpopular times, because a mentor is respectful of our positive intention and capacity to contribute. However, a mentor is mindful that people are complex and, therefore, leadership involves complex interactions. So a mentor is patient about the time it takes to sort out complicated issues.

Having a mentor is especially helpful in situations in which a person needs coaching and support from someone who knows the terrain, yet isn't the evaluator. Hearing that another person has had similar experiences or understands the dynamics is immensely reassuring, especially when we are doubting our capability. Learning how others have handled similar situations can be very helpful so that we don't have to reinvent the wheel while we are in the middle of the ride.

In my first principalship, I was offered a different kind of help by a member of the school committee. Estelle was a former school principal, and she could see what I was trying to achieve, perhaps more clearly than I, because I was so heavily entangled in the daily struggles. Estelle would acknowledge the harassment, knowingly nod with regret about the situation, and then add that she was confident that my administration would prove to be just what the school needed.

Estelle didn't inquire about my feelings. She didn't give me advice or teach me specific skills or strategies. Rather, Estelle steadfastly affirmed that, of course, I and my leadership would prevail.

Estelle was an unusual person with a noteworthy style. When she spoke, she enunciated each word and projected her voice, sophistication, and intellectual authority. Estelle commanded attention. Many people didn't seem to understand Estelle, and although Estelle rose above it, I believe she sensed their uninformed disdain. I believe Estelle empathized with my isolation and wanted to support me even though—and perhaps because—I, too, was different. I could feel Estelle's fondness for me and received tangible evidence of it when she knitted two sweaters for my newborn.

I missed an opportunity to learn from Estelle by not opening up more. With so many people speaking about what I couldn't do, I think it may have felt too risky to reveal my pain and confusion to one of the few people who had confidence in me. I was afraid I would lose Estelle's respect, and that loss would have been profound.

Time Well Spent

During my research on mentoring for my doctoral dissertation, I interviewed women administrators and their mentors. I heard about mentoring relationships that lasted for many years, through many of the ups and downs of their careers.

I have not had that experience. Perhaps it did not seem to others that I would want a mentor. My feistiness and determination may have concealed from prospective mentors my longing for a consistently supportive collegial relationship in which my growth was the focus.

In thinking about the people in my life who have mentored me for shorter periods of time, I have concluded that, for some of them, part of their interest in mentoring me came from their wish to support my ideas about leadership and education. For others, it was because I used what they said to me and worked very hard to achieve my goals.

A person who made this clear to me was Kirt, a director of career development, who helped me with my résumé when I was applying for my first principalship. I remember Kirt being very blunt with me. "This is a great résumé if you want to get another job teaching first grade." I had not expected this feedback and felt deflated, but then

Kirt told me what I needed to do to strengthen my résumé and help get me the principalship I sought.

I went home and worked on my résumé for a couple of days and called him back. "I've redone my résumé based on your suggestions. Would you be willing to look at it and tell me what you think?" We met, and Kirt helped me put the finishing touches on the document. Then he talked with me about interviewing.

I had thought that interviewing would be a strength of mine, but again Kirt gave me some unexpected feedback. "You don't look like a principal, at least not the kind most people are used to seeing. You smile too much and you are very soft-spoken. People are going to think that you will be too soft." I wanted to point out the stereotypes of a principal Kirt was describing, but I realized that he was probably right about the first impression I would make on screening committees.

"Just because I smile doesn't mean I can't be tough when I have to," I responded, probably trying to convince myself as much him.

"You know," Kirt said, "you lowered your voice a whole octave when you said that. I believed you. If you say it just that way in your interviews, I think they'll believe you too." I took his advice and, during interviews, even made a point of speaking about my demeanor before being asked. By initiating communication about my manner, I probably helped allay interviewers' doubts about my ability to be a disciplinarian when it was necessary. Of course, later I would show them that I had very different ideas about discipline, but at least my initial presentation wouldn't keep them from envisioning me as a principal.

I met with Kirt several more times, and he spent a fair amount of time with me at each meeting. Finally, I couldn't contain my curiosity. "I'm wondering why you spend so much time with me," I said. "You don't know me from a hole in the wall."

"I know enough about you to want to help you, and that is because you take my advice and work hard to use my suggestions." He continued, "Other people come in, 'yeah yeah' me, and then when they come back they complain about the same things. Have they done anything I said? No. They just want someone to listen to them whine. I feel like the time I give you is well spent."

As Kirt articulated why he was mentoring me, I realized that other people probably also had valued my responsiveness to their coaching and my willingness to work hard to improve myself. Their offers of help hadn't just come out of the blue. Learning this enabled me to seek and accept assistance with a greater understanding of what inspires mentors to make such a strong commitment.

With Kirt, as with so many people and situations in my life, I worked very hard. I always tried to be planful and diligent, yet I was able to remain open to unexpected opportunities. Having a mind-set of hope made it possible for me to respond to serendipitous situations, and my sense of possibility was further reinforced.

The Courage to Pursue Growth

I believe a mentor encourages considered risk-taking. When I decided to send the letter about swimming and self-acceptance, I hoped that trusted colleagues would support my decision. Instead, I found that colleagues who cared a great deal about my well-being were more concerned about the potential negative consequences of my act than what was to be gained. Instead of naming their fear of my being hurt, their fear about it did the talking. The message I received was "There are dangers inherent in this endeavor, so don't do it." They made a judgment about my action, based on the reaction I'd received instead of the value of what I did.

I had more courage than they did at that time. I longed for some support for the risks I took to write and share that letter with our school community. I wanted to hear someone say: "This an important letter. If you are prepared to take the fallout (and there will be fallout), do it. Do it and I'm behind you." Mentors need to support risk-taking to promote growth. In this way, mentors can offer what friends sometimes cannot.

As important as mentors and supporters are to us, we ourselves often know more than we may realize, but we must get quiet and listen. When I mentor, I encourage people to listen to themselves and pursue their passions. We discuss the possible ramifications of any endeavor, and sometimes I advise them to use another approach that would help them achieve their objectives without putting themselves in jeopardy. I work to help them think about whether the risks they are contemplating are worth taking. I urge them to explore what "feels right," and I advise them to use their courage carefully but certainly to take the risks that they believe they must.

What We Give to Each Other

In my doctoral research, one respondent adamantly resisted identifying mentors in her career, feeling that the term connoted positional power that was not reflective of any relationships she had. She acknowledged the importance of some key people in her career yet insisted the relationships were not based on a higher-up/lowerdown structure, in which one was the mentor and the other was the grateful recipient. Instead, she described collegial and equal relationships.

Many people think this mutuality cannot occur when mentors are also evaluators, because of the confusion that this added dimension will have on the relationship. Although I agree, I have mentored a number of staff members at schools where I was principal, because some teachers specifically sought me out. With them, I have developed deeper relationships because of their interest in working more closely with me on their professional development, remaining cognizant of the times when my supervisory role may have to take precedence.

One person with whom I shared a more mutual mentoring relationship was an unsuccessful inside candidate for the principalship I obtained in her school. Josie was very intelligent, sensitive, and talented, and she had been a part of the system for a long time. The superintendent told her he didn't think she was quite ready to be the principal and that she should learn from me once I arrived. Who learned the most is debatable.

Josie knew the staff, she knew the children, she knew the system, and she knew the town. As an added bonus, she knew a lot more about technology than I did. In many ways, Josie seemed to me to be the perfect candidate for the principalship, although I wouldn't have had the chance to meet her had the superintendent seen it that way.

Flowers sent by Josie greeted me when I first arrived on the job. She was up front about her aspirations to be a principal and candid about her experience of applying for the position I now occupied. She wanted to learn, and I was happy to teach her anything I could. As it became clear how much Josie was orienting me and advising me about situations at the school, I was even more delighted to reciprocate.

There are probably strategies I helped her learn, though I think she would have been able to figure them out herself. Perhaps the way I most helped Josie grow was by processing with her the events at school and the staff's reactions to my leadership. Although Josie might have done things differently herself, she got to observe what happened when I did something my way. She saw how her colleagues responded to initiatives that she and I thought made sense, as well as how I processed it all. These were the things that Josie and I could discuss as we reviewed the day's events. We speculated about how the faculty would react to a different way of leading; Josie was able to imagine reactions and then see what actually happened.

Because many of the staff were Josie's longtime friends, I imagine that she heard a much more candid version of people's reactions than I ever did. (Josie was actually in an even better position to evaluate what was happening than I was.) My reactions may have been helpful to Josie because I was new to a system she had been a part of for a long time. Sometimes we encountered difficulties when some of the staff disagreed with initiatives or reacted to a way of leading that was new at this school. Sometimes we took detours along the way or even changed our course as we obtained new information, but Josie saw that we continued to move forward.

I respected Josie's professionalism immensely. She was always interested in what was best for the children, she respected people's confidences, and her only agendas at school were to learn and to be of service to the school community. I wanted to do anything I could to assist her in reaching her professional goals.

I told her about NECEL and encouraged her to join. We discussed the relative merits for her career of attending various workshops or conferences. I offered Josie my experience as a principal and Josie was a translator, ambassador, and special advisor to me.

When it was time for our school to be evaluated for accreditation by a visiting team, I appointed Josie as the chair of the steering committee. I knew she had the organizational, communication, and analytical skills the job required, and I thought it would be a great opportunity for her to "show her stuff" in this leadership role. Of course, it did not escape me that she would do a tremendous job.

She could see that I was the kind of leader who didn't feel the need to have everything figured out in advance. I actually had volunteered for our school to become accredited, although it was not typical for elementary schools. My faith in the benefits of a self-evaluation process was confirmed, although I couldn't have predicted how.

Our staff were insightful in evaluating our school, the staff, the community, and our programs. Josie got staff members on board who might not have participated as fully had she not been there to request their involvement. Some of the teachers may have been nervous about participating in a school accreditation, but Josie knew how to make them comfortable. By the time the visiting team arrived, Josie had put them at ease.

We got rave reviews and commendations from the visiting team. Soon after, Josie obtained her first principalship in another school district. I had been very pleased to speak with that superintendent about Josie when she was one of the finalists, and I was so enthusiastic about her that the superintendent commented on the intensity of my high regard.

Josie became a different kind of principal. She once made a deal with the students of her school that if they read a certain number of books, she would dress up in the costume of their choice and spend a day on the roof of the school. Josie helped motivate the students to read more books, and she kept her promise: She dressed as an astronaut, and up she went.

When a critical letter about her actions was printed in the town paper, the outcry from the community was deafening. There were so many letters of support for Josie during the following weeks that she was close to canonization. I was delighted. She was clearly a principal with a unique way of leading, and it was just as important that her constituencies valued her for it.

My role as a mentor had been to validate her talents and encourage her to take the risks to be a principal in her own way. Seeing her do this gave me the satisfaction many mentors experience as they watch talented women and men assume leadership.

Passing the Torch and Sharing Its Light

When I mentor, I sometimes teach how to do things, like preparing a budget or writing a proposal. Other times, I share my experiences before and while becoming a principal, to give a picture of what different aspects of the job are actually like. I sometimes mentor administrative aspirants in their practica and internships; through working together on projects, the interns and I are able to combine theoretical and practical information in ways that can be useful to different constituencies in a school community. However, we spend most of our time processing events or dilemmas, with an eye toward developing and refining strategies. Seeing how the principal acts in a situation and then reviewing with the principal how it went provides insight into both people's thoughts about leadership.

In the process of mentoring, mentors benefit from hearing other perspectives, as well as from the questions they are asked. Mentors often have to clarify and expand their own understanding in order to respond to inquiries about their actions. This is an opportunity for mentors to reflect on their own professional growth. It is often very satisfying for mentors to see themselves through the eyes of people at different stages of their careers. It feels good to help other people learn and move forward, and I sometimes receive from them the same things I offer: a sense of belonging, opportunities for growth, and support for risk taking.

Good mentors are in high demand. There are many more people who seek such a relationship than could possibly be accommodated. In addition, it may be more difficult to find, in one person, all the attributes and knowledge we desire in a mentor. Although it would be a joy to have the concentrated attention and support of a mentor who offers it all, we can successfully piece together what we need from different people. I have. It's like grazing throughout the day, even though sometimes it would be luscious to have a feast.

A way that some colleagues and I have brought such richness into our lives is to meet for a weekend once a year. These colleagues are women I know from NECEL, one of whom astutely observed that we always were so busy organizing conferences and attending to all the details that we never got a chance to finish our own conversations. After our first weekend, it was clear that we wanted to ensure that this would be an annual event. In this group of women, whose ages, lifestyles, and careers are very different, we support, gently tease, and encourage one another.

Whether in a group or individually, leaders can cultivate these relationships. We can do this by carefully choosing people in whom to confide and share experiences, by listening and following up on what they have said, and by letting them know their impact on us.

Even though some mentoring relationships can go on for a long time, we must realize that our efforts to promote the growth and professional development of people we mentor may result in their departure. Teachers I have mentored have moved on to become principals, to raise children, and to pursue other careers. I believe that it is my responsibility as an educator to encourage them to take the next steps they envision. In fact, there have been times when I have suggested endeavors that capitalized on or expanded someone's talents, knowing that person might leave teaching as a result. Although it may be a great loss when they leave, I also feel pleasure and delight for them.

I feel strongly about my responsibility to help aspiring administrators—especially women—join the profession. Just as others have given to me, I enjoy being able to continue the cycle of support and coaching. It feels very satisfying to pass the torch.

Leading With My Voice

Writing this book feels like a new way for me to mentor, although it is primarily with people I won't meet. When I was just starting out, I would have loved it if people had shared with me what they had learned in their years as principals. I still find it enlightening to hear how others deal with situations similar to those in which I find myself. The knowledge of how useful it can be to share stories has kindled and fanned my desire to share my craft wisdom through writing.

The writing and publishing of this book has been a journey in itself—a journey of exploration, of priorities, of decision making. It brought for me a new level of thinking, learning, and expressing, and a new stage in my growth and evolution as a leader. One of the reasons I wanted to write this book is that I believe leaders have a responsibility to continue growing and to contribute to the profession. It was a risk, and I knew that the process of writing a book would require some of the very leadership abilities I was writing about.

I sent my book proposal to publishers and was excited when I was offered a contract, yet the realities of the potential breadth of my audience started to sink in. Believing in relational leadership as much as I do, I was naturally concerned about the possible impact of my writing on people I know or have known in the past. Four of the incongruities that could cause problems would be how other people remember the events, how they interpret what I write about the events, whether they agree with my opinions or analysis, and whether they will feel threatened by my writing the stories at all. Would I have to sacrifice my own voice so that others could continue to feel that their voices were protected?

Many authors don't mind upsetting other people; some seem to relish the uproar they create. That has never been my style. I worried about how telling my stories might affect some of my relationships and my effectiveness as a principal—specifically, that people would become afraid that I wouldn't honor their confidences, that they would find themselves in print in the future, or that our work would suffer if they didn't agree with my conclusions or commentary.

As well as being an author, I continue to be a principal, and even when I am no longer a principal, my commitment to the welfare of the school community will always make me mindful of the effects of telling stories about real people, real situations, and real relationships.

Careful examination of options and possible negative outcomes is part of effective leadership, but leaders also need to recognize when continuing to explore these possibilities gets in the way of moving forward. After I considered all the pitfalls—everything that required caution—I had to decide whether I would let myself succumb to the fears about what would happen. Part of how I moved ahead, despite my concerns, was to remind myself that accepting the potential of negative fallout from my writing is part of the modeling I do, the modeling that may inspire others to take their own risks.

As Marianne Williamson wrote:

Our deepest fear is not that we are inadequate. Our deepest fear is that we are powerful beyond measure. It is our light, not our darkness, that most frightens us. We ask ourselves, who am I to be brilliant, gorgeous, talented and fabulous? Actually, who are you not to be? . . . Your playing small doesn't serve the world. There's nothing enlightened about shrinking so that other people won't feel insecure around you. . . . And as we let our own light shine, we unconsciously give other people permission to do the same. As we are liberated from our own fear, our presence automatically liberates others. (Williamson, M. [1992]. *A return to love* [p. 165]. New York: Harper Collins)

It may not only be the obstacles outside ourselves that hold us back; it also may be the challenges of facing the magnitude of our own possibilities. I hope that by writing this book, I inspire people to value and trust their talents and strengths, to envision their own leadership, and to be emboldened to act authentically.

CORWIN
PRESS

The Corwin Press logo — a raven striding across an open book— represents the happy union of courage and learning. We are a professional-level publisher of books and journals for K–12 educators, and we are committed to creating and providing resources that embody these qualities. Corwin's motto is "Success for All Learners."